Jan Wahl

THROUGH a LENS darkly

Jan Wahl

THROUGH a LENS darkly

Adventures with Louise Brooks, Lillian Gish,
Dolores Del Rio, Jackie Coogan, Leni Riefenstahl,
Rita Hayworth, Robert Mitchum, Mae West,
Carl Th. Dreyer, Isak Dinesen & Others

BearManor Media
2009

Through a Lens Darkly:
Adventures with Louise Brooks, Lillian Gish, Dolores Del Rio,
Jackie Coogan, Leni Riefenstahl, Rita Hayworth, Robert Mitchum,
Mae West, Carl Th. Dreyer, Isak Dinesen & Others

© 2009 Jan Wahl
All rights reserved.

For information, address:

BearManor Media
P. O. Box 71426
Albany, GA 31708

bearmanormedia.com

Cover design by John Teehan

Typesetting and layout by John Teehan

Published in the USA by BearManor Media

ISBN—1-59393-311-8

To
Mark and Lois Perrier

With
special thanks to
Sig Humanski

Table of Contents

Foreword i

Introduction 1

Chapter 1 7
    Conrad Veidt Slept Under the Bed

Chapter 2 21
    The Amazing Tall Tale of *The Silent Enemy*
    and Chief Long Lance

Chapter 3 37
    Gloria Swanson Wore a Funny Hat

Chapter 4 47
    Three Puppeteers: L Starévitch, George Pal
    and Tim Burton

Chapter 5 59
    The Day I Almost Killed Garbo

Chapter 6 71
    Do You Know About Oskar Fischinger?

Chapter 7 85
    Quick Comet In the Sky: Louise Brooks

Chapter 8 115
    Comic Strips Were a Fine Art

Chapter 9 127
    Butterflies Across the Meadow: Ernest Thesiger,
    Ruth St. Denis and Paul Swan

Chapter 10 139
   A Cup of Coffee for Carl Th. Dreyer

Chapter 11 165
   The Baroness Tossed Me Out

Chapter 12 175
   Movie Stars To Meet In Heaven: Rudolph Valentino,
   Mary Pickford, Douglas Fairbanks, Colleen Moore

Chapter 13 193
   Postcards from Leni

Chapter 14 205
   Looney Tunes and Happy Harmonies: Hugh Harman
   and Rudolf Ising

Chapter 15 229
   Glamour Pusses Up Close: Mae West, Marlene Dietrich,
   Dolores Del Rio and Rita Hayworth

Chapter 16 247
   How I Became America's Best Otter

Afterword 255
   About Andrea King

About the Author 257

Foreword

Jan Wahl's essays are wondrous observations into a magic place of movies, comic strips, and books. His orbit in life has crossed paths with many interesting luminaries. A twenty-year friendship with Louise Brooks and his working for Isak Dinesen and Carl Theodor Dreyer are only a few of the fascinating adventures you will hold in your hands.

His experiences are full of passion and love. After reading them I think you'll want to rush to a library to find out more about your favorites or you'll run to a nearby video store or watch them on TCM at the next opportunity.

I am proud to call him my friend.

– Andrea King

Introduction

friends and family tell me it's time to put on paper my adventures with film folk and such and maybe explain why, though I love movies so much, I chose not to be part of that world. The answer is simple.

Having witnessed Carl Th. Dreyer directing *Ordet* was a wake-up call—filmmaking isn't for the likes of me. Making a picture book text, however, means buying a ream of good quality paper and holding a nice pen. A lot easier.

So the written word feeds me while the visual arts, movies in particular, fascinate me. A picture book of thirty-two pages is like participating in creating a one-reel short.

I can't imagine life without movies, the people that make them and the special world of comic strip art and, of course, books.

Now there are talented folk whose work I strongly admire, yet who are underrated or get a bum rap. In this book I will throw a pebble or two out upon the pond. I will make, I hope, a few ripples.

The tragic flaw of Leni Riefenstahl was that she was spellbound by Hitler—I make no excuses for it. Nevertheless, her unique documentary, *The Triumph of the Will*, preserves with brilliant art part of history.

We can't sweep it (or her) under the rug. And so I sent her a piece I titled "Leni Riefenstahl Defended—Almost," and she wrote back and so on. I felt she should have a chapter.

Recently far from flattering books on her have come out. In *A Life*, by Jurgen Trimborn, is described her 1938 visit to Hollywood. He writes, "Walt Disney, who was friendly with the Nazis, received Riefenstahl despite the general boycott." Disney, he claims, "was a great admirer of Nationalist Socialist Germany and regularly participated in meetings of the American Nazi party."

Wow. Loaded stuff. Then he continues:"Max Roach, comedy czar and Chaplin's discoverer…," and I came to a screeching halt.

I find three major errors in that small corner of a long sentence. "*Max* Roach"? "Comedy *czar*"? "*Chaplin's* discoverer"? How credible is Herr Trimborn about more serious matters, I wonder…

On a desert isle equipped with electricity so I might bring a projector, I'd be content with the output of Hugh Harman and Rudy Ising—contemporaries of Uncle Walt and supreme animators in their own right.

A Technicolor reissue of Rudy Ising's 1940 *The Milky Way* (which won an Academy Award) knocked my socks off. Hugh Harman's incredible *Peace on Earth* in 1939 was nominated for the Nobel Peace Prize. No other cartoon has received such a prestigious tribute.

These were made during their MGM period when they produced some of the best cartoons of all time—astonishingly varied in subject and increasingly accomplished. Yet before they turned forty both were gone. Forgotten. To add insult to injury, Leonard Maltin in *Of Mice and Magic*, discussing their rich and diverse years with MGM, dismisses their art as suffering from "stultifying" sameness. This though it's obvious that they especially went out of their way not to repeat themselves.

Mr. Maltin puts on a higher plane Paul Terry and Hanna-Barbera, whose main contributions are the relentless *Mighty Mouse* and *Tom and Jerry* rescue-and-chase cartoons.

Whether I met or didn't meet Hugh and Rudy is revealed within. Ditto why I hold them in high esteem.

I have also written about some of the golden age personalities I was lucky to encounter. I have left many out. Shame on me.

Here's an example or two.

On a hot summer's evening, must have been 1977, I was invited to a publishing party beside the East River. Self-important agents or authors boasted of deals and bigger deals.

I stepped out to a balcony overlooking the water. An attractive red-haired lady sat in deep shadow, adjusting a long skirt. Suddenly she called, "Hello, there. I'm Myrna Loy."

Myrna Loy? Myrna Loy! Eagerly I sat beside her.

She spoke not once about herself—instead, about the United Nations and her passion for this institution. Later, we talked about Joan Crawford, and I happened to mention that I got a fan letter from *her*. A bitter recluse, Joan Crawford had passed away that year.

Miss Loy revealed that she tried in vain to convince "Aunt Joanie" to keep busy by doing dinner theater. "They like to watch us old broads," giggled modest Myrna Loy.

And I wasn't sure. Ought I to include a New Year's Eve encounter at a Greenwich Village boarding house?

A buddy of mine, Deveren, was an actor who lived in a building where Veronica Lake also resided. She was currently a hostess at a nearby café. He was always hopeful to cross paths with her one day.

We came in the front door. Splendid timing. Here was the star—one leg in a thick, heavy cast—thump, thump, thumping down worn carpeted stairs.

Myrna Loy was a pirate

In hushed tones, an awestruck Deveren said, "Have a Happy, *Happy* New Year, Veronica Lake!"

To which she barked, "*F--k off!*"

To my astonishment, MoMA closed its Stills Dept. Sig Humanski, Marty Kearns and Scott Schutte came to the rescue where I lack illustrative materials. Scott is responsible for all the pictures in Chapter Two. Plus a warm salute to Russ Merritt who made the frame blow-ups for Chapter Fourteen.

Particular thanks are due Barbara Fischinger and Cindy Keefer who painstakingly corrected my Oskar Fischinger essay. I can't beat the drum loudly enough for the magic of O.F. You'll find more information on him on the following websites: The Fischinger Archive, www.Oskarfischinger.org and The Center for Visual Music, www.centerforvisualmusic.org.

I have more tales to tell. But, dear reader, that is for another day. Until then, I hope you enjoy the ones I selected for this book.

Now the curtain rises...

– J.W.

Chapter 1
Conrad Veidt Slept Under the Bed

I was an odd child. In my first years I was raised by grandparents in the flat farmlands of Northwest Ohio. When I was four years old, I startled my farm granny, who had asked me to pass the pepper and salt: "Have some despair and regret," I answered—giving her the willies. I was a poet without knowing it.

On another occasion right out of the blue, I declared, "Art is a ring of crap around the moon." What possibly did I mean? That art is sometimes lyrical and beautiful, sometimes not? Kids are certainly peculiar.

My first movie experience was when I was given a pass to the Christmas matinee of *Snow White*. I bought a Hershey chocolate bar and rushed down the aisle to sit in the front row. Whatever a movie was, I wanted the best seat!

The curtains parted. A bright ray of light shone down from the back of the theater. I was transfixed. A huge, gorgeous white leather book with gold lettering opened; the story began. On the screen shimmered the beautiful image of an enchanted castle. I had no notion how they did it—how the drawings moved. It was sheer heaven! When the blissful eight reels of *Snow White* were done and the curtains closed, I sat dazed, in another dimension. The Hershey bar was never eaten; it had melted in my hot tiny hand dripped all over me, and I hadn't noticed.

Later, *The Wizard of Oz*, a tasty treat—who could resist? Tuneful and merry and spooky by turns, another awe-inspiring experience. Like Dorothy, I was a farm kid dreaming; almost fatally—since I once guessed a fast way to get to Oz was through a morass of poop in the outhouse. If you got through the brown stuff, I thought, you came to a land of butterflies and rainbows. Honestly, I did. Thank goodness it remained a theory; I never tried it.

More electrifying than *Wizard of Oz* came the miracle of *The Thief of Bagdad*. Sabu was the true, the only hero, flying on his carpet, scurrying off to further adventures! There was another, who was Jaffar the dark magician, who was more mesmerizing than the Wicked Witch of Oz, who thrilled me with his incredible grey-blue eyes that could transform a boy (Sabu) into a dog baying at the moon.

And so I became a movie nut; in the farm village the bill changed three times in the week. The other set of grandparents lived in a town with two theaters; I was allowed to go to each program; movies were my babysitters. Roy Rogers in sepia, Betty Grable in Technicolor. I loved them all. Abbott and Costello and Danny Kaye were the reigning funnymen. However, there appeared a reissue of Chaplin's *The Gold Rush* which blew them away. Once upon a time it seemed movies didn't need to talk or sing. That intrigued me.

Bud and Lou and Danny Kaye worked hard with their hysterical, snappy routines and patter, yet they didn't hold a candle to

Charlie in the New Year's Eve scene at a lonely cabin in the Klondike, impaling two buns on a fork and doing a mock ballet. I simply shook with delight. Besides, Chaplin's Tramp figure is endearing in a way Abbott, Costello and Kaye could never be. I had to find out more about movies from times past.

A kind librarian in Napoleon, Ohio, let me roam freely into the grown-up section. (Or did I duck and run past her?) There was half a shelf devoted to movies…including Paul Rotha's early book, *The Film Till Now*, with superbly printed eye-catching stills from the silent days.

What glorious still caught my attention at once? It was from *The Cabinet of Dr. Caligari*, depicting sleepwalker Cesare carrying Jane up over the slanted rooftop. A spellbinding expressionistic image in black and white. I had seen a Reel-Art print of Bela Lugosi in *Murders in the Rue Morgue* and recognized those spectacular sets, haunted and strange. But the *Caligari* image hit me like a stroke of lightning; I resolved I had to become familiar with this movie. Somehow.

My town grandfather, a whimsical mortician, taught me how to type at his massive Remington and a local printer made me stationery headed "The Film Society of Toledo." (Toledo must be a sophisticated place, I reckoned.) And I typed what I considered adult letters to MoMA, asking questions. An assistant curator actually replied.

Somehow, I don't recall how or where, I located a 9.5mm English Pathé copy, a cut-down version of *Caligari*. I did dances of joy. Of course, I possessed no 9.5mm projector but I had the fantastic thing itself and laid my treasure for safekeeping under my bed where it stayed for several years.

The Cabinet of Dr. Caligari (1919)

It was a long while until I saw *Caligari* on the silver screen. After the end of WWII the Alien Property Custodian allowed the confiscated masterpiece to play at art houses along with Emil Jannings in *The Last Laugh*. Up through the clouds I rose again, although no Hershey chocolate bar was in my hand.

My first 16mm feature was, in a gorgeous Kodascope print, *The Covered Wagon*; yes, it was better than Roy Rogers. Well, collecting of any kind is a potent virus, be it matchbox covers or whatever. To have these ageless movies in the house was sublime. I mowed lawns, weeded gardens and shoveled snow, adding more titles continually.

Arthur Knight of MoMA put me in touch with Jim Card who worked for Eastman Kodak and became Curator of Film at

George Eastman House. A grownup—with whom I could talk about movies like *Caligari*, and best, about Conrad Veidt who was both Cesare and Somnambulist *and* Jaffar the Magician!

Jim and Jeanne Marie invited me to their house at 123 Marion Street in Rochester; Jim called it Cinemusée. Their fruit cellar was stocked with cans of lovely-smelling Kodascopes—Max Linder in *Seven Years Bad Luck*, Bessie Love in *Rubber Tires*, Wallace Beery in *The Lost World*, Charley Chase comedies and Max Fleischer *Out of the Inkwell* cartoons galore. I drooled.

I had sent my 9.5mm print of *Caligari* to the George W. Colburn lab in Chicago, where it was copied onto 16mm and at last I could play it at will on my trusty Bell and Howell, oh rapture. I told Mr. Card, who was my hero, that *Caligari* had been my very first acquisition; to my amusement, in his provocative book *Seductive Cinema*, he claims the same, though at the time he never mentioned it.

Here, now more than a half century later, I'm no longer a kid yet Conrad Veidt remains my favorite actor, bar none. If we can name Greta Garbo as Goddess of the Silver Screen inasmuch as no other female star can remotely match her beauty or mystery, you may ask: does Garbo have a male counterpart? Yes, yes, yes, I shout. His name is Hans Walter Conrad Veidt; he's in three films among the most famous ever made. Conrad Veidt (say it like "fight"), as we know, is the sleepwalking murderous puppet of Dr. Caligari, Cesare, who carries the limp girl up the painted rooftops; as Jaffar in Technicolor he can summon a monumental storm at sea by lifting his arms and calling, "Wind!" and as the nasty Major Strasser he deservedly gets shot by Bogart at the airport in the delicious end scene in *Casablanca*.

The Cabinet of Dr. Caligari (1919)

Now if you don't know at least one of these performances and savor it, I'm talking to the wrong person. The range of his roles was beyond measure. Often he suggested, by his glance, by the way he stood, the sinister and diabolical with a hint of the icy fires raging within.

Slim as an arrow—nay, truly gaunt—he lived on air. His grey-blue eyes were world-weary. Someone once called him "an urban Mephistopheles." This is an age when grownup films were made for grownups.

Yet just as easily he could play a saintly being, the "Stranger" in the British drama of 1935, *The Passing of the Third Floor Back*. Other mortal folk walk into a room—whereas Conrad Veidt slips in on silken feet. When you hear him mutter in *Thief of Bagdad*, "What is love? The lisping of two children in a garden!"

or that spine-tingling command of "*Wind! Whip yourselves, winds of Heaven!*," you can thrill to the uniqueness of this supreme actor.

Like Garbo, Veidt was already famous as an international star in silent films. Two years after *Caligari* he became Lord Nelson in *Lady Hamilton* (1921), then Cesare Borgia in *Lucrezia Borgia* (1922), also he was *Paganini* (1923), Ivan the Terrible in *Waxworks* (1924) and he became *The Student of Prague* (1926). In 1927 he was invited to leave Germany by John Barrymore, who wished him to play King Louis XI in the fable about the French poet and revolutionary Francois Villon, *The Beloved Rogue*. Only a brave, clever man like Barrymore wouldn't feel bested by a presence such as Connie. Giant in every sense: Veidt obliged a much-shorter Barrymore by playing his role in a stooped position.

And his performance in *The Man Who Laughs*, directed by Paul Leni for Universal in 1928, is one of the most eerie in film his-

Jan Wahl, film collector

Conrad Veidt as Jaffar, June Duprez as The Princess in
The Thief of Bagdad (1940)

tory. For Veidt managed to make Victor Hugo's pathetic Gwynplaine—with a perpetual horrendous smile carved by Spanish gypsy surgeons—into a character grotesque yet beautiful.

This is a sampling of Connie's silent work. The Laemmles thought he would be perfect for *Dracula*. But Veidt not yet comfortable in English, returned to Germany, where he was superb as *Rasputin* (1932).

A year later he exited the now-corrupt land of his birth and moved to England, where he made wonderful films. Thumbing his nose at the Nazis, he made *The Wandering Jew* (1933) and *Power* (a.k.a, *Jew Suss*, 1934), the latter opening at Radio City Music Hall. In between, he took a chance and returned to make his last German-speaking role, *William Tell*. He was held captive; it was told that he was "too ill" to travel. Fortunately he was rescued when the British government sent in their own doctor.

The same thing happened to Pola Negri when she agreed to return to Germany, and she fought to be released. Hitler had his favorites and hated to let them go.

Ironically, when WWII splintered the globe, Veidt was cast in Hollywood—on loan-out to Warners by MGM—as the perfect Nazi. Before he left England (and Korda), he played sympathetic Germans (circa WWI) in *Dark Journey* (1937, opposite Vivien Leigh) and *The Spy in Black* and *Contraband* (1939 and 1940, respectively, opposite the regal Valerie Hobson).

Conrad Veidt, wife Lily, daughter Viola arrive in US

Veidt as Paganini (1923)

At MGM (and Columbia) he was permitted to balance his roles between good guys and bad; his leading ladies were Norma Shearer, Joan Crawford and Loretta Young. Regarding his perverse character in George Cukor's excellent *A Woman's Face* (1940—the scarred face was Crawford's), he eloquently stated his intentions in playing a un-hero: "If only I can make people feel that this man, this spirit of evil, is an unhappy human being. Sick with unhappiness, the unhappiness of Lucifer, the angel cast out of heaven. If I can do it as I see it, other unhappy people will feel they're lucky in comparison. And even happy people will feel a little sympathy for him."

Conrad Veidt with feline friend (Sig Humanski Collection)

That probably sums up Veidt's basic genius. Here is a man who acted onstage guided by Max Reinhardt himself. He did Shakespeare and Sophocles and Gorky and Strindberg. Louis B. Mayer, more eager to expand the talents of Mickey Rooney and Judy Garland, loaned Connie for supporting roles. Thus, Major Strasser.

The cruelest blow is that MGM once had both Garbo and Veidt under contract. What music might they have made? She begged for the chance to work with him. It's a lost opportunity of epic proportions.

Another: In 1924 having finished *The Saga of Gosta Berling* in Sweden under Mauritz Stiller's direction, Garbo was to do *The Odalisque from Smyrna*—with Stiller doing locations in Constantinople; it never happened. Her co-star was to be Conrad Veidt.

Always known as a humanitarian, during WWII Connie gave the bulk of his star salary to the War Relief (he had become a British citizen). After *Casablanca* he finished one more film and then died of a massive heart attack, not living to see the war's end; he was fifty.

Early in his career, Veidt, the risk-taker, appeared in Richard Oswald's "Social Hygiene" 1919 features, *Prostitution* and *Different from the Others*. Titles tell all.

Upon his 100th birthday (1993), I attended an ambitious tribute, letters, artifacts, stills and posters, at the Gay Museum in Berlin. It was in honor of his courageous pleas for tolerance.

Standing before a one-of-a-kind poster, I silently wept to think he vanished, almost like a puff of smoke, as did the Stranger in *The Passing of the Third Floor Back*.

This spectacular poster declared,"*You Must Become Caligari!*"
Well—I never did.
Though *Caligari* once lay under my bed. 🔲

Conrad Veidt at home

Chapter 2
The Amazing Tall Tale of
The Silent Enemy and Chief Long Lance

The medium of silent film was less than forty years old when it died. It went out not with a whimper but with a wallop. Astonishing films were made at the tail-end. In France, Danish Carl Th. Dreyer had just made his uncompromising study of the trial and suffering of a saint, *La Passion de Jeanne d'Arc*.

In Russia, Pudovkin, Eisenstein and Dovzhenko perfected cutting, or montage, to the highest degree. In Germany, Volkov directed a film with the most mind-boggling sets ever seen before or since, *Secrets of the Orient* (or Sheherezade).

In America, a terrific silent feature appeared in 1930. It was *The Silent Enemy*, shot in the Hudson Bay region, a drama of Ojibway Indians before settlements of white men. Now almost forgotten, I find it one of my ten favorite films. Like a master painting, it never grows stale. The beauty of its camera work, the lifelike pure quality of the actors, its sweep and power caused *The New York Times* to shout, "Unforgettable!"

"Unforgettable" describes this film in a nutshell. It is a docudrama—about the role of Hunger in the lives of an Ojibway tribe long ago. Incidents in the story are from journals of Jesuit missionaries who lived among Ojibway during the 17th and 18th centuries in Canada.

The inspiring force behind the production was W. Douglas Burden, a Canadian-born naturalist explorer, remembered primarily for studies of the sea turtle in the Galapagos Islands. *The Silent Enemy* is a lost gem of moviemaking.

W. Douglas Burden, producer of *The Silent Enemy* (1930)
(Scott Schutte Collection)

The Silent Enemy and Chief Long Lance   23

But beyond all this is the incredible tale of its star actor, whose life deserves a film of its very own.

Douglas Burden was mightily impressed by Robert Flaherty's *Nanook of the North* (1922), showing Eskimo life, and his *Moana* (1926), showing the life of natives in the South Pacific. Also, he knew Schoedsack and Cooper's *Grass* (1925), about nomadic tribes in what was then Persia and the dangers on their annual trek across flooded rivers and treacherous mountains. And there was *Chang* (1927), filmed by S. & C. in Borneo, with its thrilling elephant stampede through a jungle village.

These directors opened up a fresh new genre of moving pictures, somewhat in the manner of classic photos of Northwest Indians by Edwin S. Curtis, in which past and present are intermingled in dramatic form to suggest a larger truth.

Douglas Burden felt this was a way to demonstrate to audiences the many hardships and rewards of Indian life and thus to preserve the memory of it.

With a partner, William Chanler, he interested Jesse Lasky of Paramount in distributing. After all, *Grass* and *Chang* had done well. Chanler and Burden began at once to raise the necessary funds. The film was shot on location, Temagami Forest Reserve of Northern Ontario.

Its authentic teepee village lay on the shores of Rabbit Lake, where Ontario meets Quebec. Shooting commenced in November of 1928. The finished feature was premiered in New York City, May 19, 1930. Its national release was not until August of that year. Alas, the silent film had all but vanished from the silver screen—gobbled up by a phenomenon, the Talkers.

Only Chaplin had success in releasing silent features later: *City Lights* of 1931 and *Modern Times* of 1936. However, Charlie Chaplin was still the most loved movie actor in the world.

The director of *The Silent Enemy* was H.P. Carver, who rose magnificently to the occasion; assisted by Ilia Tolstoy, grandson of the Russian novelist. Cameraman was Marcel Le Picard, who'd been on D.W. Griffith's epic *America* in 1924. He ended at the

Chief Long Lance as Baluk (Scott Schutte Collection)

bottom on the heap on such pictures as the Bela Lugosi Cinecolor *Scared to Death*, which scared nobody in 1947.

Everybody who collaborated on this unique production was inspired by the flame lit by Douglas Burden, who insisted on choosing an all-native cast.

For the role of the tribe's chief, Chetoga, he picked Chauncey Yellow Robe, nephew of Sitting Bull and hereditary Chief of the Sioux. The eloquently-spoken prolog to the film was written by him. His commanding presence assures us that we are about to witness something special.

As Chetoga's daughter Neewa, Burden found Molly Spotted Elk dancing at Texas Guinan's speakeasy in New York. As Chetoga's son Cheeka, he chose a pureblood Indian boy whose American name was George McDougall. Dagwan, the sinister medicine man, was Chief Akawanish, whose Canadian name was Paul Benoit.

The most important role, that of the fearless hunter Baluk, required an Indian brave truly noble looking. The script describes him as "the epitome of manly development." The young man they picked fits this description; he couldn't have been more perfect.

And there he was, Chief Buffalo Child Long Lance himself. His portrait was the frontispiece to his bestselling book, *Long Lance, the Autobiography of a Blackfoot Indian Chief*, just published in 1928. It was a huge success—in the U.S., in Canada, in England, Germany and Holland.

Chief Buffalo Child Long Lance was the most famous Indian of his day. Legions of admirers knew him as the "ultimate noble savage."

He was an athlete who trained for 1912's Olympics with Jim Thorpe; he sparred with Jack Dempsey. He was a writer and reporter who had been appointed to West Point by President Wilson but instead joined the Canadian Infantry. He was said to have distinguished himself in action in France—for which he won the Croix de Guerre. He was a pilot who, on his first solo flight, did three loop-the-loops. He became a much-sought-after lecturer on Indian affairs.

He dazzled all who met him by his heroic stance, his intelligence and mostly for his knowledge of Indian life and lore. I agree with Douglas Burden. Long Lance was born to be in this film.

Now comes the fly in the ointment.

Long Lance claimed to be born in a teepee in the Sweetgrass Hills, somewhere near the Canadian border. Yet his real name was Sylvester Clark Long and he grew up in Winston-Salem. His parents were born into slavery. His family on both sides was racially ambiguous. Both sides always maintained they were mixed white and Indian.

Chief Akawanish as Dagwan (Scott Schutte Collection)

Evidence suggests it was not exactly so; there was, what was termed in those days, Negro ancestry. In Sylvester Long's time in that part of the South, you were either white or "colored."

As a child (and he must have been an exceptional child) he refused to accept the barriers of the South. According to the law, with one drop of Negro blood you were legally "colored." Colored could not go to a white school.

So at the age of thirteen he ran away with a circus, having often fantasized about the Wild West. With his straight black hair and high cheekbones and copper skin, he was taken as the Indian he wanted to be. Eventually, though, he returned home to work as his father and brother Abe did, as a colored janitor in a white school. To someone like Sylvester Long, it was only a half-life.

Once again he joined a circus and, working with horses, learned to ride. He became good pals with a registered Cherokee and picked up some of the language. Returning home, he educated himself. He learned to type—something "colored" didn't do. Claiming to be part Cherokee, he applied for admission to Carlisle Indian School in Pennsylvania, the most famous Indian institution in America.

A fellow student, Jim Thorpe, soon to be called the Greatest Athlete in the World, never doubted him and remained a close chum his entire life.

Thus began the difficult trail upward. Sylvester Long, i.e., Long Lance, step by step became a reckless fibber. But he was able to live a life that otherwise would have been denied him. For when he was a youth, in some quarters, the most advanced "colored" was considered beneath the lowest white man.

He rose steadily in celebrity by his immense intellect, charm, courage, tremendous will. Despite his reckless lies and ever-changing personal history (if an authentic Cherokee ever doubted him, instantly he became a Blackfoot or a Sioux), he fooled many of the people most of the time. Long Lance the imposter became the acknowledged spokesperson for all Indians in his day.

After World War I, in which he had risen to the rank of lieutenant (not captain as he later claimed), he became a reporter with the *Calgary Herald*.

Ultimately, covering City Hall's beat bored him—no outlet for his ferocious energy. To liven matters up one morning he tossed a smoke-bomb into the Mayor's council meeting. The Mayor accepted his apology after Long Lance, laying on the charm, claimed it only a joke. The newspaper's owner didn't find it funny.

Next, he journeyed to Vancouver, where he wrote articles on the plight of Indians in British Columbia. After that, he moved to Saskatchewan, where he rallied to the cause of the Plains Indians. By now he was a much-respected, seasoned reporter on Indian matters.

Long Lance wrote a thirty-four-page pamphlet, *How to Talk in Indian Sign Language*, illustrated by eighty-some photographs of himself. It was recommended by his old pal, the athlete Jim Thorpe. He published *Indians of the Northwest and Canada* in 1924.

His outstanding gift as a journalist was his ability to draw out Native people—including the usually reclusive Chief Carry-the-Kettle, who was 107 years old. Distinguished historians praised articles that Long Lance wrote about Indians of Western Canada. More and more he became *the* advocate for Native rights.

At this point in his career he took to posing in what was his own "native" garb. The costume he carefully put together was not exactly authentic. For he sported a Blackfoot vest, a Blood

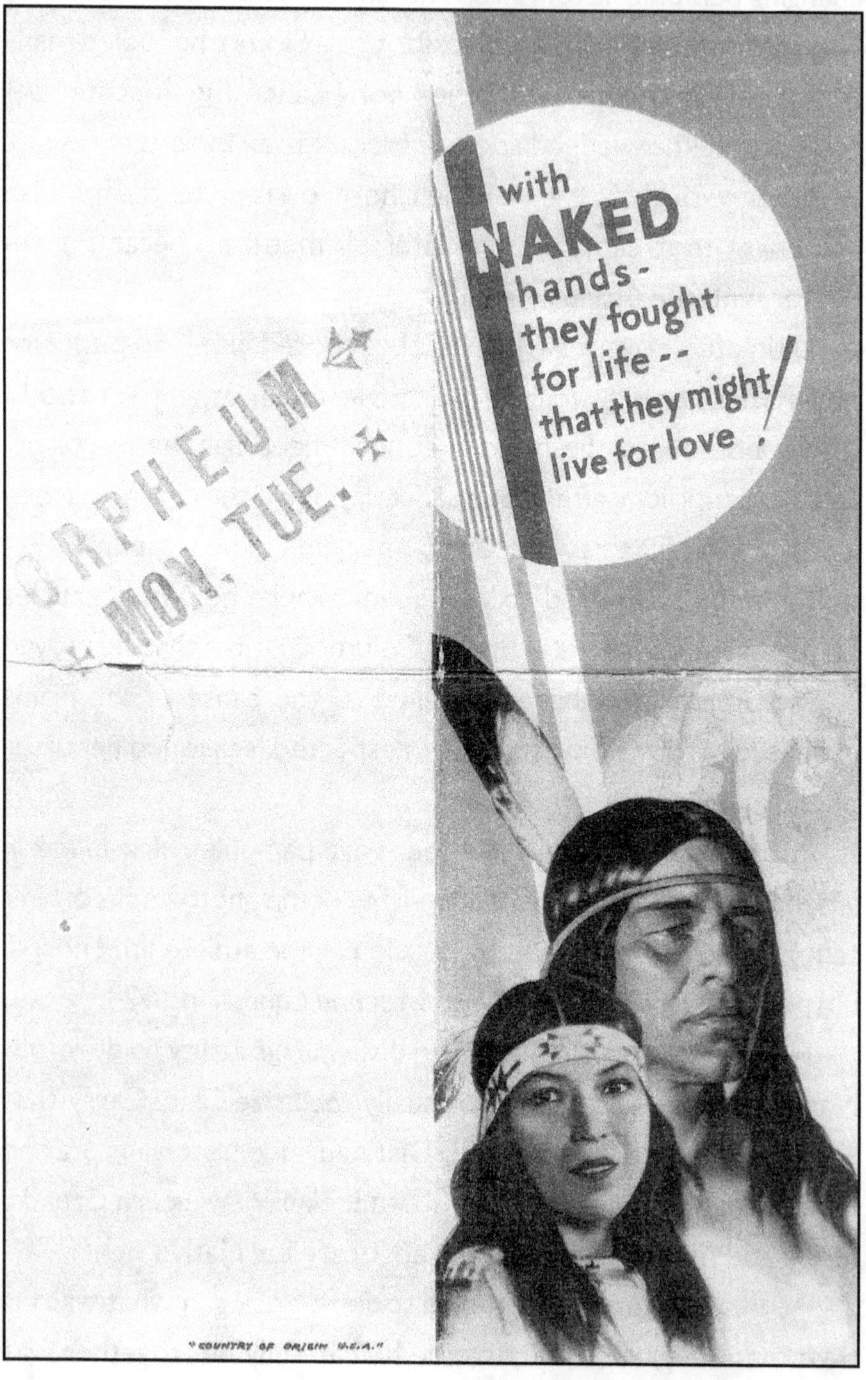
with
NAKED
hands-
they fought
for life --
that they might
live for love!
ORPHEUM
MON. TUE.
"COUNTRY OF ORIGIN U.S.A."

Indian tobacco pouch, Crow Indian pants (worn backwards) and a headdress used only in the Chicken Dance.

He tried to explain to a missionary, the Reverend Middleton, why he now had taken on the identity as a Plains Indian. He declared he had not lived among his own people since the age of eleven. By presenting himself as a "Blood," he said, it gave his writing an additional touch of interest. This was hard even for a devoted friend to swallow.

Reluctantly, the Reverend Middleton did accept this new literary identity for he felt that Long Lance might, with his expertise and gift for language, help change the prevailing negative views of Indian culture.

Next, it was on to Winnipeg. Somehow, wherever he went, his bizarre costume never received comment or criticism— such was the persuasiveness of his personality.

Indeed, Long Lance had energy to burn. Often he demonstrated his celebrated war whoop, which was said to sound like "several fire engines or air-raid warnings lumped into one (sound)…blood-curdling and exciting."

In his favorite photo of himself he is attired in splendid white buckskin, war bonnet and moccasins, mounted on a pinto pony. He was blessed with a novelist's imagination.

By this time he was famous on the lecture circuit and spoke to university clubs, to students and to civic groups coast to coast. His eagerness and knowledge of his people captivated all audiences.

At Circleville, Ohio, an enchanted crowd rushed pell-mell to the platform, six thousand strong, eagerly trying to shake his hand. The platform collapsed. As ever, he had a charmed life and was unhurt.

He was earning one hundred dollars a lecture in a period when the average American got $1500 per year. He was overly generous with his income; he gave it away to needy friends and causes.

In 1928 he published his "autobiography." It was a sensation. His popularity soared. His fascinating work had an introduction by novelist and playwright Irwin S. Cobb, then one of the best-known writers in America.

In September of 1929 Long Lance became the single non-white member of New York's prestigious Explorers Club. At the same meeting, Charles Lindbergh was only elected as honorary member. As the fame grew, his fibs multiplied by leaps and bounds.

Yet to his immense credit, at the height of his fame, he wrote a blistering article about the Office of Indian Affairs. He rightly called them to task: while many Indians starved, the Bureau was holding unspent a billion dollars in a trust fund. Here were monies, wrote Long Lance, not being used as they might have "to feed the starving stomachs of our old people who bore the brunt of this terrible thing that civilization has done."

The white man, he continued, did "surge across the West, killing their game, raping their women, giving them diseases they had never heard of, picking fights with them and trading bad liquor for their buffalo robes." The government, he went on, had "by trickery, promises and presents, bribed the Indians into signing away their rights to their reservations."

Forcefully, he then called for a reorganization of the Office of Indian Affairs and laws governing the Indians. This article naturally got suppressed and the Bureau at once went to work to bring the man down.

During the making of *The Silent Enemy*, one person had doubts regarding the true identity of Long Lance. And that was none other than Chauncey Yellow Robe, who played Chetoga, Chief of the Ojibway. There had been slip-ups in many of Long Lance's fantastic tales. Too many details of the young man's off-screen behavior seemed wrong, and Yellow Robe decided to blow the whistle.

The false chief pleaded with the old chief. He convinced Yellow Robe that, in the Carolina town in which he was raised, only two races were recognized—white and colored. This hit home directly inasmuch as the older man knew too well about discrimination.

After all, the younger man *was* an Indian in spirit. He had done his scenes stripped to the waist in 40-below weather without complaint. He had faithfully performed his own feats of derring-do. He had convincingly played Baluk the mighty hunter.

Chief Buffalo Child Long Lance (or Sylvester Clark Long), the star of *The Silent Enemy*, was admired by the Hollywood elite: Doug Fairbanks, Mary Pickford, Charlie Chaplin, Harold Lloyd fell under his spell. He was photographed with Clara Bow and Irving Berlin.

And in Hollywood he met Anita Baldwin, one of the richest women in America. She swiftly "collected" him as she collected rare Indian artifacts. For his part, he loved being adored.

It was in Anita Baldwin's library, when he was about to be publicly exposed as a hoaxer, that he put a gun to his head and ended, in 1932, a most remarkable life.

His true identity may have been a lie. Fact and fiction in his life were entwined. However he was simply living out his dream of how life might have been, if he had truly been born an Indian…for the world needs dreamers like Sylvester Clark Long, who can step out of their own skin.

Once, when masquerading as a Sioux, he made this poem:

> We respected our old people above all others
>   in the tribe.
> To live to be so old they must have been
>   brave
> and strong, and good fighters, and we aspired
>   to be like them.
>
> We never allowed our old to want for anything…
> We looked upon our old people as demigods
>   of a kind,
> and we loved them deeply. They were all our
>   fathers.

I admire the man; he's one of my heroes.

And Chauncey Yellow Robe, who, in his ancient wisdom decided to hold his tongue about the truth concerning Long Lance or Sylvester Long, composed and spoke the moving prolog to *The Silent Enemy*. I can quote it but can't give his meaningful message as well as he.

"This is the story of my people," he says. "Look not upon us as actors. We are Indians living once more our old life. Soon we will be gone. Your civilization will destroy us. But by your magic we will live forever."

Chauncey Yellow Robe, a genuine Sioux Chief, died of pneumonia soon after the release of *The Silent Enemy*. In Douglas Burden's film, as old Chetoga, he is seen toppling like a tree, majestic forever. "This is the story of my people," he tells us in his prologue. "Look not upon us as actors. We are Indians living once more our old life. Soon we will be gone. Your civilization will destroy us. But by your magic we will live forever."

Baluk the mighty hunter, as portrayed by Sylvester Long, will live forever in this monumental epic.

Chapter 3
Gloria Swanson Wore a Funny Hat

In the early 1960s, having finished a stint in grad studies at University of Michigan, I headed for the Big Apple, determined to be a published writer of books for children of "All Ages." As luck would have it, my first book was given as illustrator a world-famous artist. Straight off the farm, so to speak, supposing fame and fortune lurking around the corner, I sublet an elegant floor-through with garden at 11 Cranberry Street in upscale Brooklyn Heights. Years later, that very same brownstone was the one Cher entered in the movie *Moonstruck*.

I learned an advance on royalties for a kid's book was a miserly $500. When I nearly collapsed in my seat up at Harper & Row, it got bumped up to a thousand. I had to move swiftly around the corner to modest digs, a dingy, sunless basement flat on Columbia Heights. The day I carried boxes and bags to the humbler abode, I saw actress Wendy Hiller nimbly climb the steps next door to the home of Forrest and Wright, who concocted the musicals *Kismet* and *The Song of Norway*. Next door, on the other side, lived Norman Mailer, who, upon discovering I

Gloria Swanson, circa 1920 (Sig Humanski Collection)

wrote "sissy" books (as opposed to his tough books), proceeded to stick his tongue at me whenever we crossed paths.

This was my introduction to the dazzling world of celebrity. A lot of monumental folks were still alive at that time, many of them my heroes, and I met, or supped with, poets such as Langston Hughes and e.e. cummings, writers Susan Sontag and P. L. Travers (mother of *Mary Poppins*), Mario Puzo and Nelson

Algren, movie stars like Vivien Leigh and lesser ones too. Whee! I was on a roll.

But no one I encountered was more fascinating or more warm-friendly than Gloria Swanson. I had met her at George Eastman House at a great gathering of silent stars.

There was Harold Lloyd (who showed us at age sixty-some how he could still climb up the side of the building itself as he had in *Safety Last*, using his one good complete hand and nimbly using the other), Richard Barthelmess (who lost his voice owing to cancer of the esophagus) and other notables from the golden age of the movies.

At that time I was a student at Cornell where one of my instructors and encouragers was the author of *Lolita*, Vladimir Nabokov. Come to think of it, that was part of a golden age of writers in America as well. I picked flowers deep in Ithaca's grassy gorges (where *The Perils of Pauline* had been shot) with Katherine Anne Porter. I lunched with poet Langston Hughes at the Student Union and bummed a ride to Syracuse on a thick-snow winter's eve to drink with a glassy-eyed porcine Dylan Thomas in a half-lit seedy bar.

I took for granted that all these wonderful talents would be around forever.

And now Miss Swanson was graciously letting me visit her as she stayed at a posh Fifth Avenue address.

I put on my best and only suit. I bought it that morning on 42nd Street. $37. Gotta look swell for Gloria Swanson! But let me interrupt the scene before it starts.

Sometime later, I was with her again. She had a driver, and we crossed the bridge over to Englewood, New Jersey; she wanted to pass where she had owned a mansion in the Twenties. She mentioned Rudolph Valentino had been expected to dance the tango at a party. For that possibility she imported, *for one night only*, an entire parquet aged-wood floor from a Spanish castle. She felt it would give the best sound.

We drove through an area with handsome stately homes. "This was my property," she pointed out, narrowing her eyes as if staring down decades. "Wow, what a place," I replied, awestruck. "No, dear," she explained airily. "That's only the guest house. The main house was torn down years ago."

To me, Gloria Swanson represented the embodiment of Hollywood royalty. First time I ventured seriously in New York, she stood near Times Square among the ruins of torn-down Roxy Theater, wearing a red evening gown, being photographed. The Greyhound bus whizzed by. My life has been blessed with moments like that.

This memory was on my tongue's tip when I rang the doorbell at an impressive mansion on Fifth Avenue. She disarmed me, opening the door her queenly self. She wore an outrageous straw hat bedecked with exotic flowers of (to me) unknown origin.

"Is it too much?" she trilled, as if for expert advice from a fellow hatter—John Fredericks or Lily Dache. "Well, it makes you look taller," I mumbled. She laughed, beckoning me inside. The living room was filled, on chairs and tables, on the floor, with all sorts of paper patterns and rolls of patterned cloth, etc. She was, she said, designing a line of dresses for the younger crowd.

She pushed a few hat boxes aside. They contained, as she showed me, a variety of hats of her own making. "Usually I can stay free at the Waldorf," she confided. "I just call in advance and ask them, 'How would you like to say *Gloria Swanson* is staying at the Waldorf?' And they agree. A friend is lending me this while I finish my line."

Suddenly she rose, all petite five feet of her, this tiny dynamo, taking my left hand, jabbing it above her tummy. "Look—

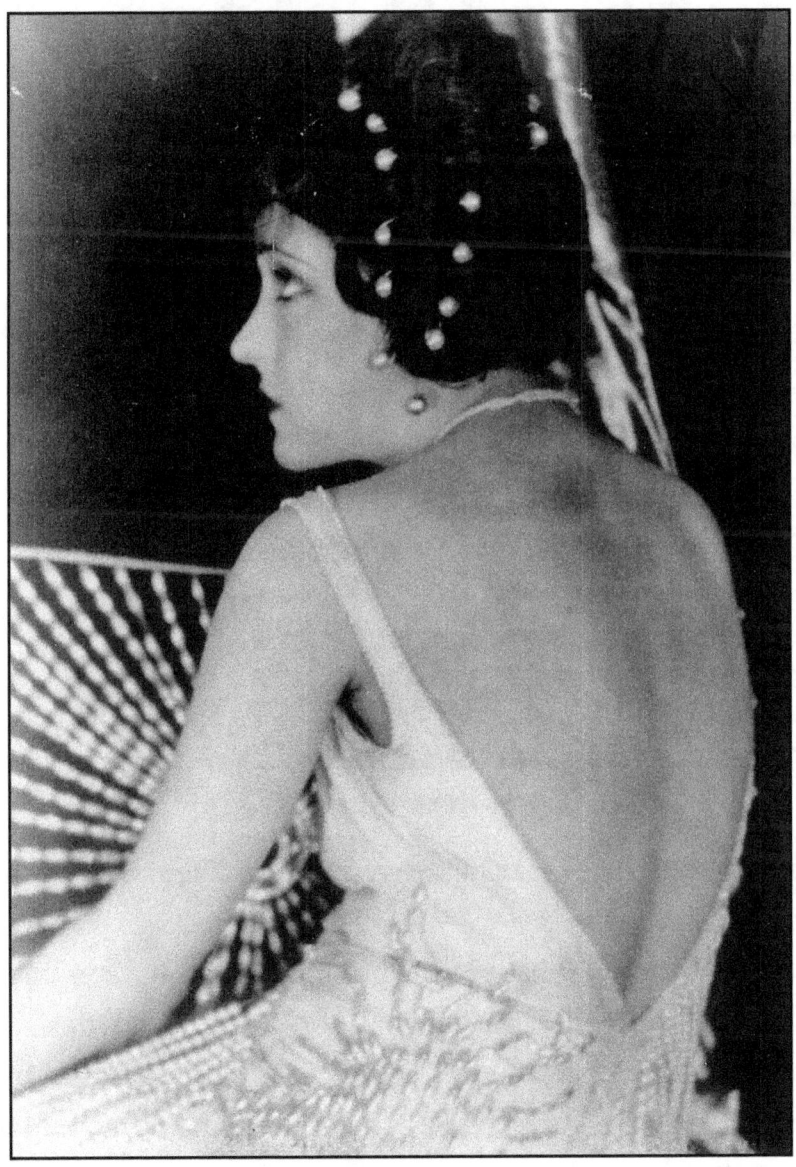

Gloria Swanson, circa 1918. I forgot to ask her to sign this.

Gloria Swanson, circa 1928

real," she declared, meaning there was no artifice to her nicely-shaped form.

I knew at once what she meant. My mother back in Toledo knew the designer and dancer Don Loper who designed Marlene Dietrich's fabulous curvaceous body, formed by a clever latex undergarment, resulting in a fantasy figure for Miss Dietrich.

No more need be said. Miss Swanson guessed I knew. She kept in fine shape by a rigorous healthful diet and lots of vegetable juices. I never got around to asking her to sign the photo portrait I brought her to autograph, so overwhelmed was I by her energetic chatter. Most enthusiastically she described the important project into which she was pouring herself.

Gloria Swanson, circa 1941 (Marty Kearns Collection)

It was not dresses or hats. It was to be a musical version of her huge success *Sunset Boulevard*, in which, with Billy Wilder's help, she was worthy of an Oscar, an Oscar she didn't get. She told me the names of the two men who were writing her musical. The names didn't click with me and I can't recall them.

After all, Swanson was an accomplished singer, as evidenced by her earliest talkies. In *The Trespasser* (1929) she introduces the song "Love, Your Magic Spell is Everywhere." It became a boffo hit. The lady could not only act and speak, she sang.

In the sophisticated farce *Tonight or Never* (1931), in which Melvyn Douglas is co-star and, most curiously, a bald-headed Karloff is her impresario, gowned by Coco Chanel and portraying a diva, Swanson opens the film by doing the end scene from *Tosca*. Even better is the charming Joe May-directed *Music in the Air* (1934), in which she sings Jerome Kern melodies.

She felt she was in good voice again and was being tutored; however, time was pressing on and one matter concerned her greatly. Paramount still had not given permission on paper to turn *Sunset Boulevard* into a musical. Don't worry, they told her—we're not doing anything else with it.

I left her that afternoon, giddy from sharing her own joy over this terrific possibility—into which she was to spend several years and her own funds.

The clock was ticking. La Swanson still looked like the glamorous star she truly was, yet she knew most likely this was her last tremendous effort. She saw me to the door as if by then we were old acquaintances. Only after I stepped out into Fifth Avenue twilight with lamps of Central Park glowing, did I remember I hoped to beg her to do her legendary Chaplin imitation.

Gloria Swanson Wore a Funny Hat   45

Swanson by Haworth (1932)

A vice president of Paramount was heard to say, "*Sunset Boulevard* isn't a Paramount!" So much did they care, just fifteen years after the classic movie in which she had given a bravura performance.

Well, she was to receive a great blow. The musical of *Sunset*, which she commissioned and gave mighty efforts to, on the very eve of its debut at an old Colorado mining town's opera house (in which Oscar Wilde had appeared), still had not gotten the official O.K.

Desperate, near hysterical, according to a Swanson friend, she made a last-minute phone call to the powers-that-be. Without apology, they informed her that she was not to get permission.

That was it.

I believe her hair immediately went white from grief. Perhaps because she could not bear to relive this episode, she chose not to refer to it in *Swanson on Swanson*.

What I remember most of all is her sincere girlish, no, her ageless excitement over a beautiful idea. She did not live to agonize over the Andrew Lloyd Webber version with Glenn Close, not Gloria Swanson, singing Norma Desmond. Too late for Gloria, whose inspiration it was, Paramount ultimately saw dollar signs in the venture.

I can only imagine how perfect Gloria Swanson might have been. I'll keep forever that vision of her in a flower-bedecked bonnet and, under it, the captivating radiance which emanated from her tiny majestic figure.

She was no Norma Desmond, a fading light—she was a woman with a future. She was going to sing Norma Desmond, Queen Kelly be damned.

Chapter 4
Three Puppeteers:
L. Starévitch, George Pal and Tim Burton

Still in knee pants, I became a magician, a puppeteer, a piano player. Anything to get out of school, which I found stultifying. I performed before PTA and church groups and once appeared onstage with Harry Blackstone himself.

But the latter episode convinced me legerdemain was not my calling. In a whisky whisper the great magician hissed at me to peek beneath the skirts of a pretty assistant to see if anything lay hidden. This was tawdry Burlesque. I was mortified.

On Saturday mornings I played piano on a radio show called *The Kiddies Karnival* on the Storer Broadcasting System. My mother's cousin Lola, the musical director, or I would accompany a somewhat older tot, Teresa Brewer. One day an NBC talent scout took Teresa, tap shoes, satin Tunic and vocal chords, away to New York City. Remember a hit song about putting a nickel in the nickelodeon? That was Teresa Brewer. Showbiz was not my thing, either.

It turned out if I identified with anything then, it was puppets. The minute Jim Card gave me a Kodascope print of the Starévitch

Frogland (1923, or "The Frogs Who Wanted a King," after La Fontaine), I got hooked. Puppet films were special!

I'd already been knocked for a loop after viewing George Pal's *Jasper and the Watermelons* in Technicolor, at the neighborhood Colony Theater during a kids' matinee. Starévitch and Pal are my kind of guys.

The third puppeteer I'll mention is Tim Burton, on whom praises were heaped for *The Nightmare Before Christmas* (1993, not long ago reissued in 3-D). But if you want something original, I'd nominate his later effort, *The Corpse Bride*. As irony would have it, the macabre yet nutty, ingenious *Corpse Bride* was superior. This time, however, reviewers pretty much sat on their hands and *The Corpse Bride* vanished.

Originality? Let me go off on a tangent.

Have any of you out there noticed how quick reviewers are to applaud an instant "classic"? This is an appellation that puzzles me. Silly nut. I thought a classic was a long-earned honor; it takes a while to elevate a work to that status. Not quite like ageing a cheese but if anything a classic improves with age.

Maybe a problem is that while art or music critics invariably try to acquire historical perspective on their particular field; most movie reviewers are not similarly educated.

They seldom recognize that movies have had a one-hundred-year history.

Movies as an art form did not start with *Citizen Kane*.

A classic is *Alexander Nevsky* or *La Passion de Jeanne d'Arc*. A classic is not exactly *The Lion King*. One thing a classic doesn't need to do is borrow. Let's stick with *Lion King* for just a minute. It borrows heavily from far across the wide Pacific—to Japan, where there are very clever animators. I'm a fervent admirer of *My Friend Totoro* and *Howl's Moving Castle*, though, brilliant as they are, they lack discipline and, more significantly, feeling. Or do I reveal I'm not of a technological era where feelings don't count? Seems to me that *Snow White*, *Pinocchio* and *Bambi*, from Disney's golden age, retain their strengths. What the Japanese have is an ability to surprise, to overwhelm us with surreal delights—not to evoke emotion.

Getting back to *The Lion King*, it turns out there was a Japanese TV cartoon series known as *Kimba the Jungle Emperor*, inspired by Osamu Tezuka. Hmm, there's an eerie connection here. Kimba and Simba? Besides the relationship between good lions and their allies—a talking bird and a wise old baboon. Double hmm. Moreover, in Tezuka's work, Kimba's nemesis is a one-eyed lion named Claw. In *The Lion King* Simba is menaced by a lion named Scar.

Not surprisingly, the Japanese have noted more coincidences. However, the bottom line is that *The Lion King* was a box office champion globally. Money wins out. Ask Harry Potter.

More post-Uncle Walt matters: and there's *Aladdin*. Would Uncle Walt have been telling his scriptwriters to borrow the villainous Jaffar from Alexander Korda's classic *The Thief of Bagdad* starring Sabu and Conrad Veidt? Let me observe that the look of all recent Disney animation borrows heavily from the Japanese inasmuch as *The Little Mermaid* (and every Disney thereafter) with human characters has them drawn as square-eyed people. An idea the Japanese got hold of forty years ago; it's more international.

Well, I've gotten that off my chest. Returning to my subject. Where was I? Oh yes, I was identifying with puppets. Go to your video shop. Search for *The Cameraman's Revenge and Other Fantastic Tales: The Amazing Puppet Animation of Ladislas Starewicz* or *The Puppetoon Movie* by George Pal. Then let the glorious wit and beauty and originality of these works enchant you in more ways than you have ever known.

To use of the French spelling, Starévitch was born in Poland in 1892. When he was a mere nineteen, he moved to Russia, where he became director of the Museum of Natural History at Kovno in 1911. Wishing to film two stag beetles close up, he realized with hot lights shining down, the battle he hoped to film between the beetles didn't happen. So he made his own insects, modeling them and moving them frame by frame. He realized he enjoyed the possibilities in animation. Soon his *The Grasshopper and the Ants* was being seen by Czar Nicholas's little boy.

Starévitch preferred puppet films to live acting. "Actors," he proclaimed, "always want to have their own way."

When the storm of the Bolshevik revolution disrupted his life, Starévitch, like many Russian artists, escaped to France. There he converted a barn into a studio. His world consisted of butterflies, grasshoppers, frogs, storks, fish-bones and toys—delightfully fantastic yet accurate in their movements.

In many films, such as the prizewinner of 1923, *Voice of the Nightingale*, Starévitch employs miraculous, tinted pastel colors. This fable, with his own daughter Nina and his puppets, is a true gem with impressive delicate effects.

He managed painstakingly to finish a black-and-white feature, *The Tale of Renard the Fox*. A dozen years in the making (from 1928 to 1940), this gorgeous film is an hour long. The subtle movements—an animal's chest heaves with emotion, tears spill slowly—are nothing short of remarkable. The costumes are every bit as intricate as the costumes by Christian Berard for Jean Cocteau's *Beauty and the Beast*.

No detail is insignificant for Starévitch. The pity is that one viewing is never enough: there's too much happening in every frame! His films require intense concentration. His master-

Starévitch: *The Tale of Renard the Fox* (1940)

piece, a three-reeler called *Fetiche the Mascot* from 1934, is hard to describe. At midnight, a toy dog literally visits the Devil in desperate search for an orange for a sick child. Fish-bones dance, turnips quarrel with onions, shoes become flying ships through the air. It's a dark feast, worthy of E.T.A. Hoffmann.

Starévitch: *The Tale of Renard the Fox* (1940)

The pursuit, in which the cloth dog Fetiche is followed by these creatures and toy gendarmes, concludes this weirdly irresistible, haunting child's dream.

Ladislas Starévitch kept laboring on his beloved puppets until his death at age eighty-three in 1965; his last films were in Eastmancolor.

I believe George Pal, a Hungarian born in 1908, always used color, beginning with Gasparcolor in the early Thirties. He had been an architect, then did sets for mighty UFA (as did Alfred Hitchcock), and then at last went to Holland where he made advertising shorts for Philips.

He created what he called Puppetoons. (Unlike Starévitch's, which were constructed of cloth, paper and wire, Pal's were carved from wood.) His *Ship of the Ether* (1934) manipulates figures of glass. His wood puppets, though stylized, are highly expressive. In England he did films for Philips and Horlick's.

The charm of the Puppetoons, coupled with jazz or popular music, won Pal a contract at Paramount. These brightly-Technicolored one-reelers include *The Sky Princess* (1941), a most whimsical fairytale; *Tulips Shall Grow* (1941), a powerful anti-war piece in which bombing raids are invoked suggesting the destruction of Rotterdam; and two charming adaptations from Dr. Seuss, *The 500 Hats of Bartholomew Cubbins* (1943) and *To Think That I Saw It on Mulberry Street* (1944). Pal also adapted, in his inimitable style, another children's story, one by Paul Tripp, *Tubby the Tuba* in 1945.

Pal had steeped himself in the culture and lore of music by African Americans, including that of Duke Ellington. He did a joyful series about a boy "of color" named Jasper and ended his

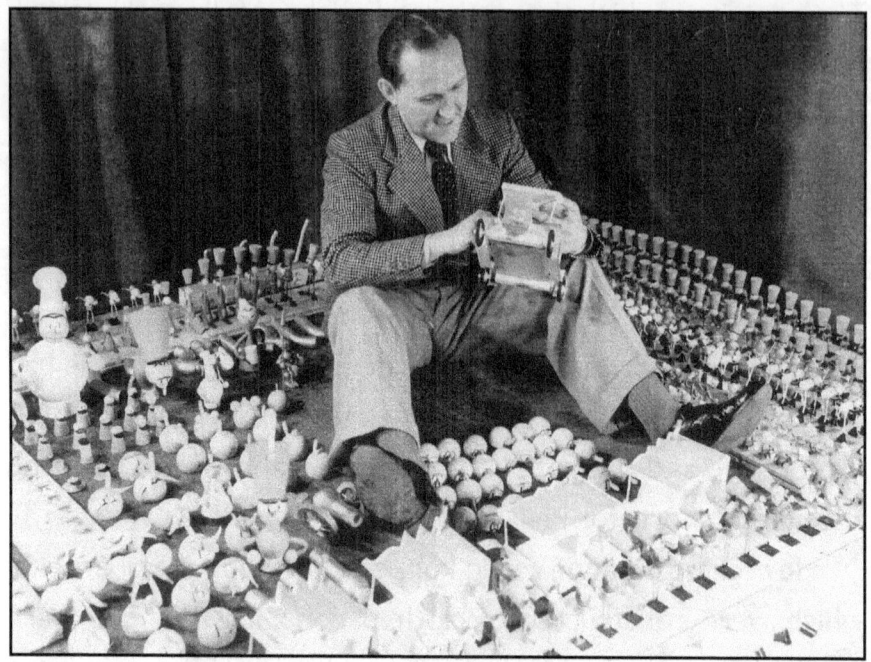
George Pal and animated pals (1937)

George Pal: *Together In the Weather* (1946)

Three Puppeteers: L. Starévitch, George Pal, and Tim Burton

Puppetoons for Paramount with the legend of *John Henry and the Inky Poo* in 1946. The shorts became too expensive to continue and today he's better known for his live-action features, *Destination Moon* and *When Worlds Collide*.

Through science fiction, Pal could employ puppet animation for what we call special effects. Better still, he returned to puppetooning for sequences in his *tom thumb* for MGM in 1958. Russ Tamblyn was the tiny hero bedeviled by both Peter Sellers and Terry-Thomas.

Of course, with his puppet films, George Pal did not get rich. Nor did Starévitch, whose films were shown in Paris on Saturday mornings. Starévitch and Pal are artists of vision and integrity, each with a lifelong commitment to making unique shorts. If they borrowed from La Fontaine or Dr. Seuss, they informed their audiences. The style and substance of their works are absolutely unique.

Let's think about Tim Burton, whose "poetic fusion of Christmas and Trick-or-Treat," to quote one reviewer, his *The Nightmare Before Christmas*, evoked such an eruption of hosannas. For starters, its hero Jack Skellington is a character right out of the Frank Baum *Oz* books—he's Jack Pumpkinhead. The basic rhyme scheme and tone echo Clement Moore's poem, "The Night Before Christmas." Moreover, the storyline is not far from Dr. Seuss's *The Grinch Who Stole Christmas*.

It's claimed that Tim Burton has made a cinematic breakthrough. Why? Because he made an animated puppet film?

Tim Burton, born in 1960, fares better with live action. The first reel of *Pee-Wee's Big Adventure* is fresh, funny and foolish. And so is his fable, *Edward Scissorhands*, although the character

Tim Burton portrait by Kevin Eslinger

The Corpse Bride (2005)

owes much to the German *Strewelpeter*. Actually, Burton's finest puppet is Johnny Depp, who is the wistful Edward.

Obviously a fascination as a child had to be the cartoons and horror films that Burton saw on TV.

For puppet originality, I nominate his *The Corpse Bride*. Totally off-the-wall, too perverse and obscure for most audiences I fear.

A daring thing altogether. A worthy tribute to his mentors and geniuses, Ladislas Starévitch and George Pal.

So what's his reward? A box office flop.

A Footnote: Back in Holland, Pal's protégé, Joop Geesink, made more puppet advertising shorts for Philips in what is tongue-in-cheekingly called Dollywood, promoting with wry wit radio, TV and light bulbs.

Pal's wooden puppets, all of the ones lovingly saved, were destroyed by a fire to his home. I wonder what happened to Starévitch's delicious creatures.

Chapter 5
The Day I Almost Killed Garbo

On the cover of *McCall's* magazine in 1950 was printed an eye-catching photograph of Greta Garbo. Happy, beaming sheer joy itself, confident—a rare depiction of the fabulous beauty, the Divine Garbo. The occasion? She was, after many false starts, about to appear in a new movie, *The Duchess of Langeais*, to be directed by Max Ophuls, camerawork to be by James Wong Howe and her favorite, William Daniels, both of whom made glowing screen tests of the legendary lady. It was to be in Technicolor.

Everything got set in motion; then, disaster. The producer for the project, Walter Wanger, shot the lover of his wife Joan Bennett (as newspapers put it nicely) "in the groin." Wanger off the picture, co-star James Mason demanded his fee upfront. Boston bankers failed to deliver. Project kaput.

Garbo had another tantalizing chance to return to the manner she wished, four years later, as Penelope to Kirk Douglas's Ulysses in a spectacular project to be directed and written by G.W. Pabst. Another dream vehicle. Ultimately, Pabst and producer Dino de Laurentiis did not come to terms. Pabst withdrew, so did Garbo, who was replaced by luscious Italian Silvana Mangano. (It would have been the year of years for de Laurentiis, since he also produced *Mambo* with Mangano and Fellini's *La Strada*.)

Following these horrendous fiascos, Garbo withdrew, doomed thereafter to wander the streets of Gotham, walking endlessly from shop to gallery to hardware store.

Garbo-sighting was a sport the most jaded New Yorker thrilled over. A friend of mine ran the book department at B. Altman's on 34th Street. On his knees, he was arranging stock on a bottom shelf when the most beautifully gloved hand in the world (his comment) reached down. "Dear God," he said to himself, "let it be Garbo." It *was* and she said in that low, unmistakable voice, "Have you no closet shop here anymore?" His mind went blank. What was a closet shop? Where Altman's sold mothballs?

Here is another friend's story.

This far-sighted fellow was making his way along East 67th Street and happened to bang his rather prominent nose on a tree. Laughter pealed out from across the block, sounding just like Garbo when Melvyn Douglas falls off the chair in a café in *Ninotchka*. It *was* Garbo, who sighed, "Life is tough."

Acquaintances, long-time dwellers in the city, shared choice Garbo happenings. I doubted I'd ever have one of my own. I hadn't been in New York more than a few years. The Lord moves in mysterious ways. Hang on.

When I was in my teens, Garbo took U.S. citizenship. *The Toledo Blade* hailed her on the front page in bold letters: "Nice Niece." Indeed she was, never another like her. She was a living immortal. What was eerie about her was that when she shimmered upon the silver screen, you could do the impossible. You read her mind. She

Greta Garbo, new MGM star (1926)

was that astonishing. Those long-lashed, expressive eyes, that terrific brow of marble purity—she didn't even need to speak.

When she did speak, that throaty voice with a beguiling accent hit you in the solar plexus. "Garbo Talks!" was MGM's hoopla for her first sound picture, *Anna Christie*.

My friend June Brown heard her at George Cukor's house declare, "I want some nuts." Total silence in the room. Somehow, with those words, Garbo summed up the total wisdom of the Universe. It wasn't what she said, it was how.

It is probably a curse to have such a gift, to say nothing of consequence and elevate it.

One gray, ghostly, twilight afternoon in December in Gotham, I confess that I nearly killed her. Upon my oath I swear it.

Garbo by Haworth (1932)

Garbo as Marie Waleska (1937)

It was the week before Christmas, no snow. About five in the afternoon the sun was lowering and the sky pewter-colored. The moment is etched in my mind forever. It was 1967.

Not dressed for a momentous occasion, I, hapless flower child that I was, wore a cheap windbreaker and had bolted from a framing establishment called Raymond & Raymond at the corner of Madison and 53rd. Anthony Quinn and inamorata, the tall, stately British actress Margaret Leighton, were having a lovers' quarrel in the shop. Embarrassed to be witness to the scene, I stepped out into the sooty, bracing winter air. I wished to clear my mind and soon was at 53rd and Park.

I swear to you, the oddest thing: a message was delivered into the pit of my stomach. Sharply, it called: "Don't move, dummy! Garbo is coming!"

I can only liken it to standing on railroad tracks as a kid in the farmlands of Ohio, feeling, ten miles down the B & O line, an electrical surge of energy as the daily streamliner approached. Obediently, I faced toward Fifth Avenue, which was west. A good half-dozen minutes elapsed. Finally, *she* came, no bigger than my thumb at first. I was frozen to the spot. My nose began to run. Unmistakably Garbo. Like the parting of the Red Sea, other pedestrians did not hinder my view as she came toward me.

You figure it out...surely it was proof of Garbo's odd power. Here she was, out of movies for over a third of a century, fated until the day she died to be hounded by photographers—even in 1990, when she was taken three times a week for her dialysis, mortally ill, newsworthy to the end.

On she came! Wearing a heavy, elegantly-cut cloth raincoat with matching hat, carrying two heavy parcels by the handles,

Garbo in *Two-Faced Woman* (1941)

one on each arm. Steering right toward me as I numbly stood mesmerized.

My lonely days in Gotham were not for naught. I now was about to meet, face to face, the Living Legend. And me only in a cheap windbreaker and my nose running! Ah, the mystery of it. As she loomed closer, I saw she was still a unique beauty, somewhat weather and age worn. A fine spider's web of tiny wrinkles had brushed against that splendid face. The excitement was too much. Nose dripping, I reached into my pocket.

Did that startle her? She realized she'd been spotted and, startled as a hare in the hunt, she lunged recklessly. She darted into Park Avenue traffic against a red light.

I gasped in horror. Cars and taxis were about to crush her. I closed my eyes…I have killed Greta Garbo, the most famous movie star of all time!

Me, who worships her as no other. Me, to whom that name is utter heaven. Garbo as Camille, Garbo as Queen Christina, Garbo as Ninotchka. I'll go down in history as the one who caused her to be killed.

But, no. Fate was kind. Like an enchanted hare or cat or squirrel, she made it past treacherous traffic. Vanishing into the twilight of a cruel city.

I blew my nose and wept. I've seen Garbo! I've seen Garbo! Crystal bells rang out, not Christmas bells, just my own. The miracle was I had sensed her minutes before she appeared. There's no way to explain it. Wise, seasoned New Yorkers nodded their heads when I told them that, yes, I had a special Garbo experience.

Garbo lived almost a quarter century after I nearly killed her. Forever walking, walking. And today we know where she went

Garbo as Queen Christina (1933)

walking and why. Only after she left this earth did we know why. Garbo, to kill the pain of being ousted by Louis B. Mayer who had tricked her into tearing up her contract, spent her days making, with care, a hidden, cozy place of refuge.

Youthful herself when she left MGM (only thirty-six), Mayer, the mogul of MGM, knew with the coming of WWII monies her films earned abroad were to be curtailed. His solution was to concentrate on young true blue Americans such as Van Johnson, June Allyson, Judy Garland. The older crowd (William Powell, Joan Crawford, Myrna Loy) was soon to be cut loose. Garbo was told she might be rehired after the war.

While waiting for the return to films that never happened, she designed handsome carpets for the floor. The furniture was Louis this and Louis that, the vases Ming. She had impeccable taste. The paintings galore were the most charming Renoir (of a child—surprise: she loved children and doted on her niece's infant. Garbo hid toys under chairs where only a babe crawling on all fours could see). There was an excellent Alexej von Jawlensky. And works by van Dongen and Rouault.

There were books aplenty, leather-bound. All came to light as Sotheby's auctioned off Garbo's immaculate collection. This was no empty-headed lady.

Many of the twenty-six films are on DVD or can be viewed on TCM. I defy any film to beat the last moments of *Queen Christina* (1933), directed by Rouben Mamoulian. It was a project she fought hard for. Christina of Sweden was a character as enigmatic and mysterious as Garbo herself. Garbo was fascinated by her.

I have studied Garbo's sketches from research she made in Stockholm—suggestions for costumes, architectural details. At the end of the film (the real queen journeyed to Rome where she would spend the rest of her days in the vast Vatican Library), Queen Christina has abdicated. She flees the country with her lover, the Spanish envoy (John Gilbert). Before boarding the ship, the Spaniard is killed in a duel and Christina decides to take him "home."

The camera floats across the deck to where she stands at its prow gazing over the sea, until her fantastic face fills the entire screen. Fills it up until you get goosebumps. As I had when on a New York street I encountered her stupendous presence.

That day, her face quickly said to me: Let me have my own thoughts at last.

Just let me be!

Chapter 6
Do You Know About Oskar Fischinger?

You never heard of Oskar Fischinger? Shame on you. To sit through a half-dozen brief Fischingers is a mind-blowing experience you have denied yourself.

Oskar Fischinger's story is not as tragic as Van Gogh's. Or is it? After finishing a masterwork, *Motion-Painting No. 1*, at age forty-

Oskar Fischinger with panel from *Motion Painting No. 1* (1947)
(Fischinger Trust, courtesy Center for Visual Music)

eight, thanks to his "benefactor," the Guggenheim's Baroness von Rebay, who dismissed it as "little spaghettis," he was never to receive funding again for a major film.

In 1952 there was one more film, only a TV commercial for "Madman" Muntz, a car dealer. He lived twenty years after *No. 1*, five kids to raise and a wife who probably had to cook stone soup. He is one of the great artists of the last century.

O.F. was born at Gelnhausen, Germany, in 1900 and was the first serious artist to choose to create paintings or drawings in the film medium. The poet Vachel Lindsay said movies are Painting in Motion. The silent film he deemed "space measured without sound." It was 1922 and he was thinking of such works as the German revolutionary, expressionistic *The Cabinet of Dr. Caligari*—in which everything, including actors, was painted.

I like that term, Painting in Motion! Of course, it's more than that. Film is composed of light, movement and sound. And was so

O.F.: *Studie No. 7* (1930-31)
(Fischinger Trust, courtesy Center for Visual Music)

even in the silent period. Silents had musical scores and noises (wind effects, bells, whistles and such). Often, they had color tints.

The painter Fernand Leger, with the help of an American in Paris, Dudley Murphy, made a short film in 1924, *Ballet Mechanique*, using eggbeaters, cut-outs, whatever pleased the eye. Top photographers also experimented in movies in the Twenties: Moholy-Nagy, Paul Strand and Man Ray. These little films are intense and mind-boggling. If you blink, you miss some amazing images.

Great films, be they short or long, are not given the status of a great painting or photography print. Don't ask why. Critics and museums are slow to catch up. Crazily enough, a lithographic poster of a movie (*King Kong*, for instance) can bring a thousand times more money than a genuine original print of any important artistic title. Go figure.

Now I feel even the most devout movie lovers have not paid just due to one of the most innovative filmmakers of them all. They'll scream about Tex Avery, but neglect the name of Oskar Fischinger.

If his work is known in a large way, it's because he inspired the first part of Disney's *Fantasia*—the Bach Toccato and Fugue as scored by Stokowski and performed by the Philadelphia Orchestra. To catch the eye of the beholder, Disney's artists converted his abstractions into violin bows leaping, arches stretching and rocks falling.

A common person can grasp the beauty of a crazy-quilt or the widening circles from a pebble tossed into a stream or a Fourth of July display of fireworks—so why not painterly abstraction? O.F. was the inspiration for *Fantasia* itself. Early on, he wished to do an abstract rendering of Stokowski conducting the

Paul Dukas "Sorcerer's Apprentice." Instead, this became an elaborate ode to Mickey Mouse without Fischinger.

What's left of Fischinger's conception is part of the Bach piece, and halfway through the film a comic interlude when the shy soundtrack is introduced. To put it mildly, O.F. was dismayed with the interpretation of his drawings. He left Disney in a huff—just as strong and stubborn as Walt himself.

Now in 1921, when O.F. was twenty-one, experimental filmmaking was uncharted territory. The first effort shown to the public (in April of that year) was Walter Ruttmann's *Light-Play: No. 1,* a play of light on various colored filmstock spliced together to give the illusion of changing colors. It's true that Germany was in serious decline after WWI; however, the arts were definitely thriving: Paul Hindemith and Kurt Weill and others in music and an explosion of painters and playwrights—and filmmakers such as Murnau, Lang and Pabst. After *Caligari,* the deluge!

By the mid-Twenties, Fischinger was pursuing his lonely career full blast; his work displays much emotion. He was influenced by Hindu mysticism, dreamscapes and music, all blending into his consciousness.

In 1927 he made a journey by foot, some 350 miles, from Munich to Berlin. With his 35mm camera, he recorded the journey, often merely a frame or two—snatches of landscape, sheep and cows, studies of gypsies or villagers or farm folk, cloud patterns, a roadside cross. In 1928 and 1929 he earned money doing effects for commercial features, including Fritz Lang's sensational *The Woman in the Moon.*

O.F. was supporting his abstract work partly by tying them into commercials. As George Pal did a few years later, only at the

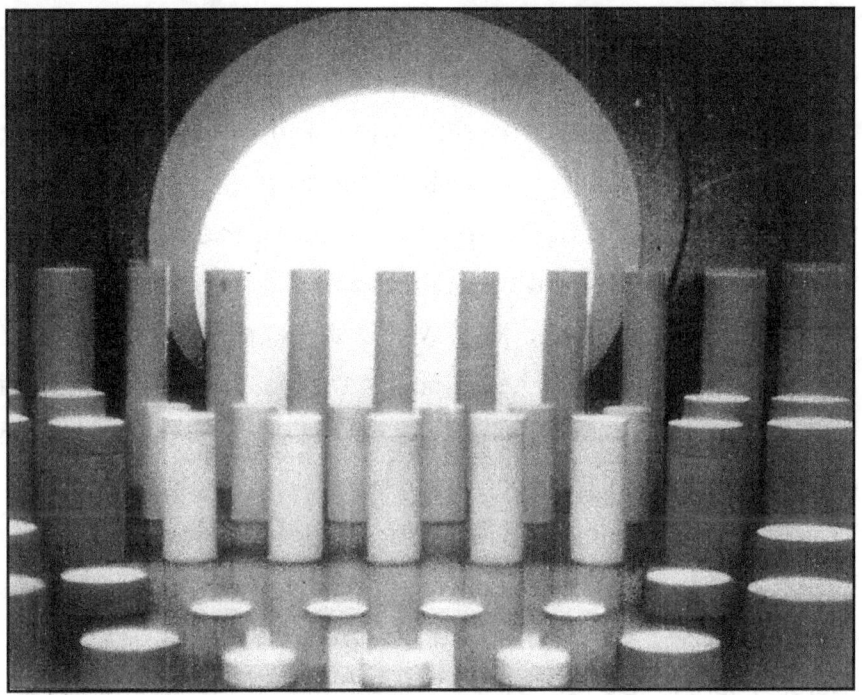

O.F.: *Composition In Blue* (1935)
(Fischinger Trust, courtesy Center for Visual Music)

very end of the reel was the sponsor's name or product revealed. The sound medium was perfect for Fischinger. He took popular recordings, a fandango or foxtrot, or maybe Brahms, and with circles, staffs, curving lines illuminated the music. He had to pay fees beyond his means. For "The Sorcerer's Apprentice," he could only buy one side of the 78 recording. This extraordinary film was left unfinished.

(By chance in the States one year earlier, 1930, the Roxy Theater's conductor, Hugo Reisenfelt, produced a one-reel version of the Dukas with live action and puppet animation; it was designed by William Cameron Menzies.)

A series of black-and-white studies were popular in Berlin. O.F.'s *Study No. 7*, set to Brahms' "Hungarian Dance No. 5," it is told, convinced future experimenters Len Lye and Norman McLaren to follow in his footsteps.

About this time, he married his cousin, Elfriede Fischinger, who thus became Elfriede Fischinger Fischinger. To my delight, sixty years later, Elfriede became a much-loved friend. My mother was exactly the same age as Elfriede and they in turn became telephone chums. O.F.'s jolly widow's specialty was a kind of Berliner hot-dog soup. There's such a thing as taste memory and I can taste it to this day. Elfriede was an artist, interested in textile design, and immediately became one of his assistants.

Just as sound enhanced his work, color in the form of Gaspar Color (he was a co-inventor) was used by him with tremendous effect in *Kreise* ("Circles," 1933), *Quadrate* ("Squares," 1934) and *Muratti Marches On* (ditto), the latter becoming a hit, an international delight, in which Muratti cigarettes walk and glide and strut in time to Bayer's "Doll Fairy."

O.F.: *Allegretto* (1936-43)
(Fischinger Trust, courtesy Center for Visual Music)

This was a huge success and my guess is the most wonderful advertising short ever devised. The "cigarettes" were actually wood sticks covered in thin paper.

The famous Dutch documentary director Joris Ivens took O.F.'s films to Moscow where they were enjoyed. Moholy-Nagy showed them with his lectures at the Bauhaus. Oskar was getting around in high places.

Then, he topped himself with the spectacular Gaspar Color *Composition in Blue* (1935), in which brightly-hued three-dimensional boxes move about in an imaginary blue room.

But in Germany this was a dangerous period for an avant-garde artist: it was not proper German art. According to Elfriede, overnight in Berlin, gypsies, beggars, drug dealers, prostitutes, Jews, homosexuals simply vanished from the streets. Degenerate artists were next in line.

It became known that Oskar's work was, according to Nazi thinking, "contrary to the spirit of the times." Also, Oskar refused to fly the Nazi flag from his window. Yet in 1935 *Composition in Blue* (a print was smuggled out of the country) was declared the "biggest sensation" at the Venice Film Festival. It was denied distribution by the German authorities.

One print each of *Composition* and the *Muratti* film somehow made their way to the U.S., where, at an L.A. art house, Ernst Lubitsch saw them. The crowd stomped its feet, whistled and demanded the two shorts be re-shown. That was enough for Lubitsch, who was presently head of production at Paramount. He invited O.F., who gladly accepted. Elfriede lingered behind briefly—hiding at the back of the Fischinger family drugstore in Gelnhausen Oskar's prints.

One copy of each of the sound films was secretly shipped abroad by Paramount. As Elfriede boarded the train from Berlin, she read the headline of a newspaper: *Sick Art*, it declared. Oskar and Elfriede got out in the nick of time.

At Paramount, he was given an office with two German-speaking secretaries, and nothing to do. So he went home and began to paint in oils and watercolors. Heretofore, he felt such painting was "static" or "old art." Yet he must have reasoned that animated films are comprised of hundreds, nay, thousands of separate works of art. He'd made a dozen or so charcoal drawings in the early Thirties and was familiar with Klee and Kandinsky and Feiniger. Eventually like them O.F. was to have paintings and drawings at the Guggenheim and other worthy museums.

At last Paramount had an idea: Oskar would provide a color interlude for a Jack Benny/Martha Raye/Burns & Allen feature based on a radio theme: *The Big Broadcast of 1937*. Bad luck—Lubitsch was now out as head of production and the director Mitchell Leisen (arguably one of the best directors on the Paramount lot) was not enamored of Oskar and his interlude; Oskar wanted it in color. The compromise was at that time to film it in black and white. Oskar, in 1941, with the help of a grant, was to buy back what he called *Allegretto*, and in 1943 totally remake it in color.

Oddly enough, *The Big Broadcast of 1937* (made in 1936) has Stokowski conducting the same Bach "Fugue" we see later in *Fantasia*. O.F. had suggested they collaborate. Hmmm and double hmmm.

By a miracle, O.F. had another chance with a major company. For MGM he was to make an abstract short called *An Optical Poem* (1937), using paper cutouts suspended on unseen sticks

Painting by Oskar Fischinger (Jack Ruttberg Gallery, L.A.)

and wires. To MGM's credit, they released it, but Fred Quimby, better known for his association later with *Tom and Jerry* cartoons, axed any further Fischingers.

Oskar painted while waiting for the next miracle to happen. Then came an offer from the Devil in disguise, Uncle Walt.

The family was in dire straits, though they got relief through the European Film Fund and now and then a hundred dollars from such admirers as Orson Welles. Oskar climbed aboard the Disney caboose at $68 a week. Otherwise, he and his family might have faced deportation.

O.F. had contacted Stokowski since his Berlin days, and also when both were at Paramount. He suggested their doing a "concert feature." Thus, he was shocked to find the distinguished conductor proposed it was his own idea to Disney—including using "The Sorcerer's Apprentice."

For about a year, prints of Fischinger shorts were constantly shown to the Disney artists and his influence is there in the "Pink Elephants on Parade" number from *Dumbo* and in *Saludos Amigos* and *The Three Caballeros*. O.F. was given the task of animating the Blue Fairy's wand in *Pinocchio*; he was reduced to special effects.

In *Fantasia*, the best one can say is that during the Bach Tocatta and Fugue and during the Intermission's comic relief of the soundtrack revealing itself to the audience, it is never pure Fischinger. Rather, it's ersatz Fischinger. Furthermore, Uncle Walt wondered if O.F.'s colors were "too gypsy."

Another outcast, squirreled away in the special effects department, was Mickey's true papa, Ub Iwerks, who had left Disney a decade before to invent a Mickey rival, Flip the Frog.

On the day the German army invaded Poland, some prankster on the staff pinned a swastika on Oskar's door. After O.F. left Disney, he was at a low, low ebb and soon came WWII. Oskar was designated an enemy alien.

Elfriede had to stretch that stone soup further and further. Sometimes, the family actually had cake, becasue the German

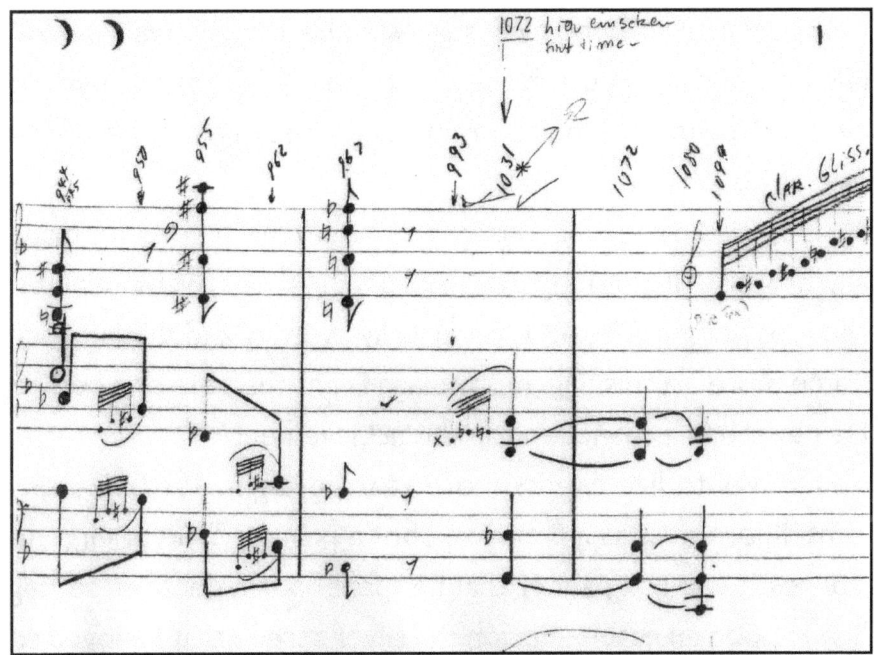

Handwritten music time sheet by Oskar Fischinger
(Courtesy Elfriede Fischinger)

cook for Junior Laemmle (and George Cukor) would bring a plate of leftovers.

Fischinger was to have animated a jazz section of Orson Welles' aborted project, *It's All True*—music to be by Duke Ellington and Louis Armstrong. Unfortunately this interesting project was abandoned by RKO. An enterprising Elfriede made clothes, was a babysitter and knitted sweaters. (One was sold to a Mrs. Merrill, who turned out to be Bette Davis.)

On the positive side, O.F. made his most memorable film in the Forties, thanks to the Baroness Hilla von Rebay of the Guggenheim, who became enraptured with his work. With the stingiest of terms now it was possible for him to finish the sublime *Motion-Painting No. 1*, which is set to Bach's Brandenburg Concerto No. 3.

The Baroness (who even suggested he leave his wife and five children, declaring no artist should be encumbered) told him the film was "awful" and took away his Guggenheim grant. He had to pay for his lab prints himself.

O.F. will be remembered for this film even if he had not made anything else. It's his longest work, running about twelve minutes, and is painting-on-Plexiglas continually evolving and shifting, each frame more astonishing, more magnificent than the one before. He never had a chance to top this achievement.

He was to live twenty more years, dying in 1967. He saw himself foremost as a filmmaker, not a painter. Due to circumstances, it was as a painter that he spent his last decades, setting his work on an easel—not on the silver screen that he loved so dearly. His paintings belong in the same exalted company as Klee and Kandinsky.

Oskar Fischinger constantly developed. It is shameful that we were denied more films by him. Still, the existing ones are magical. Each image, every frame, is a work of art.

He also invented an instrument he named the Lumigraph. It's complicated to describe. Basically, by means of hand movements, colors are drawn in the air. His notion was that this instrument might be used in any home, like a piano or synthesizer. The Lumigraph exists today at two archives where it is played before rapt audiences.

After her husband's death in 1967, Elfriede devoted herself to carrying his art around the world. With the late William Moritz, whose dedication to O.F. was phenomenal, the two went from country to country with the light-shows of the Lumigraph and the films, including a presentation at the Louvre.

Elfriede was planning to travel with her daughter Barbara to Germany in 1999 when she suddenly died, age 89. I had hoped to join her in Frankfurt. I miss her cheery voice and robust good humor.

I am forever grateful to my friend Russell Merritt and to Elfriede especially for introducing me to this genuinely great artist who makes my life richer. I am dazzled, I am spellbound, whenever I project him.

An interesting comparison could be made—two active minds working separately—showing parallels between the work of Oskar Fischinger, his abstract charcoal drawings and black-and-white films. And the early work of Georgia O'Keefe. Especially her own abstract charcoal drawings that she sent to Alfred Stieglitz at his gallery 291 for approval.

Not only that, she commented at the time: "I have," she said, "*the idea that music could be translated into something for the eye, the idea of lines like sounds.*"

One can only wonder what these two stupendous artists might have said to each other if they had met. Oskar Fischinger actually did what Georgia O'Keefe only dreamed.

Chapter 7
Quick Comet In the Sky:
Louise Brooks

Often called the "Lost Star of the Twenties," my friend Louise Brooks once was known to millions. She dazzled as a bright comet in the Hollywood sky, too soon forgotten. That is, until found again by Jim Card of George Eastman House and Henri Langlois at the Cinémthèque Française. I was there as a student when the rotund Langlois leaped to his feet shouting, "There is no Dietrich! There is no Garbo! There is only—"

At that point down came, suspended on wires, a giant photo of Louise taken in Paris in 1930 at the time of *Prix de Beauté*. "Louise Brooks!" he finished.

And the living Louise Brooks walked onstage, hair near-gray, tied in a severe ponytail. She said a few words in her odd flute-like voice, then let the Time Machine, a movie projector, restore her to youth and glory.

Not long after, Kenneth Tynan wrote an essay on her in *The New Yorker* and that glorious face, in its late Twenties prime, became the symbol of the Twenties. It was a too-late time for her because, by the late Fifties and Sixties, Louise Brooks was living in a tiny flat in Rochester, New York, as an avowed hermit. Her diet

Louise Brooks (1926) (Marty Kearns Collection)

was entirely gin, tea and oyster crackers. She lived on $5,000 a year given by one of her lovers.

I first met her when I was a student in Copenhagen. Though she was past her days of fame and fortune, people in the street guessed at once she had been somebody. But who?

Time and drink ravaged that startling beauty. Pedestrians stopped to stare in awe. Was she, maybe, Clara Bow? Those remarkable piercing eyes, that special aura that surrounds people of importance was still evident.

One of the most popular and long-running of comic strips, *Dixie Dugan* (1928 to 1962) was inspired by her vibrant persona, by her life as a showgirl, by her face. Hordes of women had copied her bangs that had been inspired by dolls from Japan. Pola Negri wore them too, so did Colleen Moore, yet Louise Brooks somehow made them her own. The first person who suggested the hairstyle for her was Sydney Guilaroff at a New York salon.

Anita Loos, the author of *Gentlemen Prefer Blondes*, called her the most beautiful of all "black-haired blondes." When Louise Brooks died in 1985, the eloquent tribute by Leonard Maltin on *Entertainment Tonight* was deserved, for though Louise Brooks is not a name as celebrated as Barbara Stanwyck or Bette Davis, definitely it is a name given more glowing status in the final reckoning. Her heyday may have been shorter and Barbara and Bette may have made more movies. Furthermore, their names were above the title and in her American work Louise had second billing—after W.C. Fields, Wallace Beery or Adolphe Menjou.

However, Louise Brooks is a name like that of Lillian Gish or Greta Garbo or Brigitte Helm or Asta Nielsen—more myth than mortal. One of the goddesses.

I feel lucky to have known her. Yet she was not easy to know. Without a doubt, she was the most complex, most baffling, the brightest person I have known. She may have shared intelligent and sparkling insights, but she could be fiercely angry and sharp-tongued. Then, just perhaps, apologetic. If I look at her movies, mostly *Beggars of Life, Pandora's Box, Diary of a Lost Girl* or *Prix de Beauté*, I marvel at what she suggested onscreen—despite a disappointing life.

Photoplay, February 1927

Louise Brooks, James Card and Jan Wahl at the Danish Film Museum, July 1957

As I write this, I glance up on the wall where I've hung a framed note from the lady; in big bold red crayon she scrawled

> I am sorry
> for writing
> that mean letter
> Merry Christmas
> Louise.

On the back of the frame I put the mean letter itself, dated December 19, 1960. I had sent a gift that I thought might be useful: a signed portrait of Ruth St. Denis. Louise had once been one of the Denishawn Dancers; in the same group was someone she held in high esteem, Martha Graham. For some reason, the picture irritated the heck out of her, and as she informed me, she hurt her arthritic fingers tearing it to pieces.

This is how we met: I took time off from the University of Michigan to be amanuensis, or scribe, to Isak Dinesen (whose real name was the Baroness Karen Blixen). "COME—AM DYING—WISH TO DICTATE LAST TALES," the great author had cabled and I left my scholarship, sold the first and last auto I ever owned, and bought a ticket to Denmark. The author of *Out of Africa* wants *me*? That adventure did not turn out well. I learned from Isak Dinesen, and soon enough from Louise, that great talent does not always mean there is a lot to be admired on a mere mortal level.

Maybe it's a curse. Life and art are poles apart.

Well, there I was in Copenhagen at any rate. Years before as a student at Cornell in Ithaca in Upstate New York, I often took the bus to Rochester. Old movies were my passion and at George Eastman House, Mr. Card made my movie dreams come true. In fact, because of the availability of treasures from the vault, Louise Brooks had moved to Rochester. Fairly late in life she realized film may indeed be an art form; it's not just something she flung her youth away on. So, years later, removed from Hollywood and a too-short career, she grew to respect her own films while film archives were beginning to re-evaluate her.

She arrived with Jim Card in Copenhagen. The Danish Film Museum was planning to honor her. So was the Cinémathèque in Paris. I agreed to escort her about Copenhagen, a city I dearly loved. So there I was, knees a-tremble, ready to show the town to Miss Brooks. From the start she called me Junior, her pet name for me thereafter.

Louise without bangs (1927)

"Um, would you like to see the famous Botanical Garden?" I asked this mysterious person. The body was heavier from decades of drinking, the famous bangs gone and the long hair, dark with gray streaks, tied in a ponytail.

"I didn't come for the flowers," she snarled.

"There are pretty good museums," I said feebly.

"Museums? I *hate* them!" she snapped, eyes blazing.

"Would you just like to stroll around?" I asked, instantly knowing this was an error. Dumb and dumber. We're wasting time, those eyes told me.

That afternoon, I learned that Louise Brooks could reply to what you were thinking and it made me uneasy.

"Have you had lunch?" I tried.

At last I made sense—she gave me an odd look. "I haven't...eaten," she replied.

I had saved up money for such a possibility; I suggested a charming restaurant called Seven Small Homes.

It was about three in the afternoon. The place would be empty. Seven rooms, each decorated in a different cozy style. Whatever might occur with my companion, midday diners will be gone. "Middag" was the Danish word for luncheon. No audience in the event she made a scene. For I had a premonition one was in the offing; I must be on my toes.

We chose the Norwegian cottage room, mostly since it lay near the entrance. She was bored with walking and wanted to sit. I pondered the fancy menu.

"What would you like?" I gulped. I had enough kroner to feed her, perhaps a cup of coffee for myself. My stomach rumbled at a furious rate. I lived on bread and cheese for a week preparing for this event.

"Junior, you order!" she insisted. Stars, even former stars, are above such matters. I had never tried Lobster Thermidor—wasn't exactly sure what it was. She glowered at a formal waiter who took the order.

We talked, about what I no longer recall, although I know she sat like a tightly-coiled steel spring. Watch out, Junior! Finally, the food got served. Our elegant waiter laid it out before her in his best manner. So *this* was Lobster Thermidor. I drooled at the

Louise by Eugene Robert Richee (1926)

sight. The waiter skimmed over the carpet to fetch my cup of coffee as if he had tiny wheels on the bottom of his shoes.

It happened. The thin spring uncoiled. Louise Brooks took the platter and without delay dumped it on the floor. The waiter, who kept his eye on us, returned to clean up the mess briskly. He made no eye contact with the lady, no words passed between them.

Now he brought on a silver tray what she truly desired: a bottle of gin compliments of the café. "For you, madam." And he disappeared.

This was her nourishment of choice. The intelligent fellow read her mind. It was my introduction to the twilight zone. Miss Brooks was baffling. Fascinating. Scary.

I suspected she always lived on some radar level other humans don't fathom. And, thus, began our long, often exciting, bumpy relationship. For more than twenty years I received a hundred letters or so from Louise Brooks, besides surprise wires or cards. My favorite is a telegram, dated June 22, 1961. I must have been back in Toledo; it simply reads;

> SCREAM SCREAM SCREAM
> SCREAM SCREAM LOVE
>   LOUISE

When in a more maternal mood, she sent me excellent homemade fudge. What a delicious treat it was! Sometimes there would be apologies for a foul mood, mostly not. A funny letter starts: "Dear Stinkpot." I sent her books found in musty old bookshops or some knick-knacks or photos to please her. Her letters were signed "A Fearful Sinner" or "Brooksie" or "Loulou" or just "Lou."

Louise, new Paramount star (1925)
(Sig Humanski Collection)

The letters were filled with flashes of wisdom and wicked descriptions of famous personages. Dancing with Fatty Arbuckle was like floating inside a huge doughnut. Isadora Duncan, the dancer who grew a bit rotund at the end of her life, was described as shaking like a bowl of Jell-O.

She described an assignation with Chaplin at the Astor Hotel in 1925. Wary of catching a social disease, he dipped the family jewels into iodine. Naked, he rushed across the room—in front of him his "little red sword."

She claimed that Rudolph Valentino's sallow complexion made him photograph better than he actually looked. He was totally neglected at the party at Gloria Swanson's. He sat glumly at the foot of the stairs, unnoticed. This, though the entire party was built around Valentino, according to Miss Swanson.

Who to believe? People came to see his spellbinding tango and did not pay attention? Was Louise hinting they preferred her Charleston?

The images Brooks raised in her letters are unforgettable. In one, she revealed, "Unlike most of my letters which are pre-written in my head, this one will have to write itself." In the letters she was honing her new art. For we both hoped to be published.

Slowly, painfully I went from published author of short stories and film pieces to become the budding author of a novel optioned by Macmillan, and at last became an author of books for children. I encouraged her; she encouraged me.

For six years I lived in a gloomy basement in Brooklyn Heights, a room with a bath and a hot plate. I lived on the hopes that someday my books might support me. Meanwhile, the domicile of Louise was a spartan furnished flat at 7 North Goodman Street in Rochester.

Now I believe that, more than anything sensual, it was our common goal, writing, that kept us in touch. I helped pull some of her pieces together, combining ones on Garbo and Lillian Gish to form a coherent essay that I submitted for her to the British magazine *Sight and Sound*. The editor, Penelope Houston, bought the piece. I have the receipt for payment which in dollars was $72.63. Please put Miss Brooks' name only on this article, I suggested.

With this encouragement, Louise worked in earnest on the book she decided she'd call *Thirteen Hollywood Women*. She had destroyed the pages of an autobiography she had labored on, *Naked on My Goat*. My editor at Macmillan, Charlotte Painter, said

Louise as "The Lily" (1926) (Sig Humanski Collection)

she had interest in publishing Miss Brooks; however it took the actress a quarter century to finish the one hundred pages of what was eventually *Lulu in Hollywood*.

Along the way she wrote me on April 13, 1976, "Only you ever sent me toys that please me. It is our common love of being ten and believing in fairy tales. But I am an old woman who can play house on my idle way to death. You are a young man struggling for fame and fortune. It is time for you to put your toy life away and face your past and write it in a novel."

At times she rejoiced in the success of some of my books. Nevertheless, she had the need to bat me down. After I dedicated a book of stories, *Youth's Magic Horn*, to her in 1978, I made no more attempts to ask for her blessing. After all—when I had sent along one book I was quite proud of, her reply was: "I prefer my old green-covered *Wizard of Oz*." Ouch. In her view, I should have finished the novel.

My guess is she grew bored once I found my path—which was primarily to write for kids. No longer was it necessary for me to write that novel. In 1968, when I moved to Mexico, in protest of Vietnam, we continued to correspond. Alas, I would get no more tasty Brooks fudge!

Her essays began to come out in small magazines. Steadily, her importance was reevaluated, especially as Lulu, in G.W. Pabst's terrific *Pandora's Box* (1928). There was a glowing reception for her slim but powerful book in 1982.

Back in Toledo, in the middle of one night (before *Lulu in Hollywood* got published), my father was awakened by the telephone. "Who is this crazy cursing woman?" he asked. "She wants you to send a photograph!" Louise wished to use for the book a copy of my Steichen portrait of her taken in Hollywood, August 1928 for *Vanity Fair*. Capt. Steichen told me when I bought it in 1960 I was the first person to purchase this remarkable portrait. Even here, the eyes look haunted. Her special demons are with her.

The humorist S.J. Perelman made a rhapsodic, warm tribute in the February 22, 1969 issue of *The New Yorker*. Calling it "She Walks in Beauty," he deemed Loulou immortal. "I am not dead yet," she told me. So how can I be immortal?" Nevertheless, she was pleased, and wrote him to thank him on the 4th of March. On the 10th of April, Perelman wrote her from his Bucks County farm. He wrote, "Your performances in pictures always gave me such pleasure, your vivacity and beauty were so exceptional, that they stamped themselves indelibly on my memory; and when, in writing, that particular piece, I was trying to convey that special quality, my recollection of you returned with great vividness. I hope this disclosure doesn't diffuse you with embarrassment. It shouldn't. I'd like you to believe that you created the same universal effect on my whole generation of moviegoers."

It was a long and generous letter, and near the close, he mentioned that the entertainment world (of 1969) was "dominated by such pallid apologies for womanhood as Jane Fonda, Tuesday Weld, and the like." The contrast between them and Louise, he concluded, "is startling." More so the Paris Hiltons of today.

What happened? Why did Louise Brooks vanish so swiftly from the silver screen? And why are we now, sifting over who has come and who has gone, endlessly fascinated?

Louise Brooks was born in Cherryvale, Kansas, in 1906. She left Wichita, where the family had later moved, to join Denishawn, the dance troupe headed by Ruth St. Denis and Ted Shawn. She was only fifteen and the year was 1922. In that same young company were a number of dancers who were to revolutionize modern dance: Martha Graham, to whom "Loulou" was devoted the rest of her life, Doris Humphrey and Charles Weidman.

Briefly, she had the notion to become a dedicated dancer also; she went on tour with Denishawn in 1922-23 and attended its summer school in New Hampshire. Soon, however, she got busy doing other things, learning etiquette, being seen at the most fashionable cafes and nightclubs, improving her speech, and dressing in the height of fashion.

She wanted it all. She hobnobbed with big bankers and brokers and, now and then, less important people such as movie folk. She was given the chance to join the *George White Scandals of 1924*. She didn't mind breezily informing George Gershwin that he wrote only one good song for the show. It was "Somebody Loves Me." She was carefree and careless and having fun. What else mattered?

Lavished upon her were ermine coats and all the fabulous trinkets an outstanding showgirl gets from admirers. Because she was a trained dancer, she won a specialty spot. And she worked hard at being the perfect flapper. "Ours," she said, "was a heartless racket."

Even better than being in the *Scandals* was being a Follies Girl. Glorifying the American Girl, Flo Ziegfeld called it. "I am a dancer—not a chorus girl," Brooks informed the showman. Duly noted. So by the summer of 1925, when she was eighteen, in the twentieth edition of the *Follies*, often called the most outrageously lavish of them all, she was the center of attention with a very hot Charleston, for which she got raves. Headliners in that memorable show were the beloved Will Rogers (whom Brooks considered a hayseed) and W. C. Fields who, she felt, had a classier act. As always, Brooks quickly got bored.

She'd been scrutinized by Walter Wanger from Paramount. By this time all major studios were out in California, although Paramount also made pictures at Astoria, Long Island.

That same year, 1925, she was signed to a five-year contract. To her this was simply a lark. Her first movie of importance was aptly titled *An American Venus* and got released on January 31, 1926. Anything was possible.

Caution to the winds!

At the beginning she worked at the studio by day and performed at the *Follies* at night. She posed for undraped art photos and a minor scandal erupted. When reporters asked why she did it, she replied that when she posed she was on the first rung of the ladder of success. Now she was on the second rung and would not do it again. The truth is the higher she would climb, the farther she would fall. But she didn't know it.

Headstrong and impetuous, merrily Louise Brooks played at being an actress. She appeared with most of the top actors and directors Paramount could offer. In 1926, it was *It's the Old Army Game* with W.C. Fields. In 1927, *Rolled Stockings* with James Hall and Richard Arlen. That same year, the Long Island studios closed and she was whisked away to the sunny climate of California where, in 1928 (loaned out to Fox), she was directed by Howard Hawks for *A Girl in Every Port*, in which she co-starred with Victor McLaglen. The same year, William Wellman directed her in her best American film, *Beggars of Life*, in which she dazzled Wallace Beery and Richard Arlen.

To one's surprise, even in lesser fare like *Love 'em and Leave 'em* (1926), Brooks makes her mark; she can't help it. She steals the show. If she sat off-camera waiting for her call, she would slouch nearby, idly reading a book. Yet, something happens the instant she steps into any scene: she is the focus of attention. By the sheer force of her unique self—her heartbreaking beauty, her awesome dancer's grace—her vitality is unforgettable.

Once she had entered a set, she changed it. She lit up with an incandescent glow. You might say this is the Brooks curse. She was doomed to be the center of it all even if she didn't take herself seriously. It was more than her energy or bobbed hair. Why do we linger at one painting more than another? What is perfection? She had it but worked hard at throwing it away.

There she was, living a fake life in glittery Hollywood. Compared to New York City it was less fun, for she missed the east coast clubs and parties, the music and stage shows. Then in 1928, after completing *The Canary Murder Case*, in which she appeared with William Powell (she was the throttled thrush), something momentous happened.

The German director G.W. Pabst, who belongs in the high pantheon of directors that include René Clair, Vsevolod Pudovkin, Carl Th. Dreyer and a select handful, asked her to come to Berlin to be Lulu in *Pandora's Box*. The idea of going to what was the most fascinating city of the Twenties struck her like lightning. She took the next ship to Germany.

Impulsive, rash as ever, it didn't matter to her that she might be throwing away a contract with Paramount. Millions of girls would have given their eyeteeth to be a star in Hollywood. Apparently, that didn't faze Brooksie for two seconds. Meanwhile, the silent film was in its last days and studios were tooling up for the big conversion to sound. She was off on the S.S. *Majestic*, snapping her fingers at Paramount.

While she was en route to Europe, Flo Ziegfeld sent her a shipboard cable. He was about to put on a musical entitled *Show Girl*, to be made for her expressly. In fact, she herself inspired the original magazine story by J.P. McEvoy. The boyfriend she was traveling with, the owner of the Washington Redskins, whimsically cabled a reply: "NOT INTERESTED," and he signed her name. Party time!

Show Girl became a Broadway success, and immediately became a (long-running) comic strip by John H. Streibel. Shortly thereafter, the strip's name was changed to *Dixie Dugan*. Louise Brooks never collected a penny.

Going to Berlin meant disaster for the Hollywood career, yet the part of Lulu, destroyer of men, was the part she was born to play. It's one of those silent films…*Napoleon* and *La Passion de Jeanne d'Arc* and *The Gold Rush* and *The General* and *Faces of Children* and *Crainquebille* (the last two by Jacques Feyder) and *Floating Weeds* by Ozu…that are ageless.

No other film of its era dares to be so truthful about the power of sex. Lulu is an enchantress, a creature who, with childlike lust and innocence, destroys those around her. Ultimately she pays the price; on a misty London Christmas Eve, Lulu, now a prostitute, picks up a sensitive-looking threadbare young man. Obviously, he's no cash customer; however she invites him to her attic room. "I like you," she says, and slowly coaxes an embrace. He is drawn to her but struggles within himself. He is Jack the Ripper. A knockout ending for this moral fable. Out of Pandora's Box leap those things that follow or precede war:

Dixie Dugan by John Streibel (circa 1951)

Death, Disease, Jealousy, you name it. Elements let loose in society's decay.

As Lulu, Brooks is incredible—she's a smoldering torch yet icy cold. The director, Herr Pabst, warned: "Be careful or you will become Lulu." Somehow, she failed to listen to his advice. After a jolly nonstop sampling the wares of naughty Berlin, nightspots and the day spots, she sailed back to New York and more parties. Paramount sent a message demanding she come back to Hollywood to shoot scenes for the talking version of *Canary Murder Case*. Pronto. The message got pitched into a wastebasket.

By returning, she might have mended the rift with studio bosses and would have salvaged her career. After all, she had walked out. However, she had a perfectly fine, slightly shrill speaking voice, having taken diction lessons to get rid of the Kansas twang.

Many silent star contracts got scuttled in a mad rush to the new medium of Talkies. Despite the economic horror of the Crash, from 1928 to 1930 theaters throughout the country wired for sound. Some stars from Europe, Emil Jannings and Conrad Veidt among them, left, unwilling to cope. Pola Negri and Vilma Banky remained, but had heavy accents. Many American stars' voices did not record like voices their fans secretly imagined. Chaplin and Garbo were hesitating to enter the new medium. In

Garbo's case, MGM feared fans would not respond well to her Swedishness. And Chaplin felt his kind of comedy was based on pantomime; he kept making silent movies.

Louise did not worry about putting her slim feet on the third step up the ladder of success. Instead of returning to Paramount for a talkie *Canary*, on impulse she was Europe-bound again. Pabst relayed that French director René Clair wished to make a film in Paris, *Prix de Beauté*. This appealed. Off she went!

However, soon as she landed, she learned that René Clair pulled out of the project; money was unavailable. But Pabst had an enticing project up his sleeve: *Diary of a Lost Girl*—why did he keep thinking of Louise? *Diary* is another moral fable in which she plays an exotic symbol—quaffing champagne, dancing her head off—yet, unlike Lulu, the girl, Thymiane, gets a happy ending.

Suddenly, after the completion of the Pabst film, all signals were "go" for the in-limbo *Prix de Beauté*. An accomplished Italian, Augusto Genina, substituted for the great René Clair; Pabst himself visited and perhaps supervised the carnival scene (or perhaps not, depending on who is telling). The dialog (very spare) was in French with Louise's voice dubbed in.

In less than two years, Louise made four superior movies: *Beggars of Life*, *Pandora's Box*, *Diary of a Lost Girl* and *Prix de Beauté* ("Beauty Prize"). These films guarantee her immortality.

The Genina is my favorite; its entirely fresh and no-studio-bound style compares to another classic, the Siodmak-Ulmer-Wilder *People on Sunday* (1929), which has a documentary approach to ordinary people and their daily lives. For *Prix de Beauté*, the director borrowed Dreyer's master cameraman Rudolph Maté, who did *La Passion de Jeanne d'Arc* and was to lens *Vampyr*. In the case of Lucienne, who wins the beauty prize, the giddiness of fame is too much. The end is outstanding, its pathos and tragic turn of events underscored by the superb music of Wolfgang Zeller.

In the Genina, once more Brooks' body movements, glances, smiles are so eloquent you are forced into the story by her radiance.

The price Louise paid for not making the dialog scenes in *Canary Murder Case* was immense. One thing is certain: William Powell (as Philo Vance) was like Ronald Colman and also Garbo: it turns out their voices enhance their image. A very minor actress, Margaret Livingston, artfully filled in for Louise as the voice of the Canary. The fact that Brooks herself wasn't actually speaking is nicely disguised. The bosses at Paramount had their sweet revenge. It was said, "The Brooks voice is not suited for major roles in talking pictures."

However, William Wellman, who remembered her as a definite asset to *Beggars of Life*, was willing to break the blacklisting and hire her for a role in *The Public Enemy*. Imagine! Jimmy Cagney meets Louise Brooks! Once more she followed a whim: instead, she chose to party in New York City.

For years the mythology is that she was offered the role taken by Jean Harlow. Nevertheless, another source states she was offered only a bit part—as "Bess" (who is nowhere in the finished product). So here is the problem: what is legend and what is not? Louise corrected a lot of facts in *Lulu in Hollywood*, as well as adding half-truths of her own. Louise's honesty was an inner matter. That is what counts.

Public Enemy was the last chance; after it, she was given nothing of value. The best she got were two low-budget Westerns—

one with Buck Jones, one with a younger buck named John Wayne. Now she left movies without regret. Like Colleen Moore, she was the quintessential flapper; flappers died with Wall Street's egg and the Great Depression.

For a brief spell she had a dance act and later (*sans* bangs) was a salesgirl at Macy's hat shop at $40 a week. She'd played that role in *Love 'em and Leave 'em*. Mostly, she drank gin and brooded over ups and downs in her rollercoaster life.

Did I say earlier she sat off-camera and read "idly"? She became self-taught, learning to think, really think hard. At last the

Louise's hand-made Valentine for Jan Wahl, Feb. 10, 1962

Motion Picture Classic, October 1927

intelligence simmering inside her exploded. In the dinky miserable one-room flats she was to inhabit for the rest of her days, she read Proust and tried to set down on paper the life she threw away.

After the move to Rochester, she fell asleep in a chair smoking a cigarette, and set fire to the place. She joined the Catholic Church and drank with her priest and kept writing.

The writing sparkled with a kind of brilliance. On June 21, 1961, she wrote me: "Chaplin showed me that movement is the foundation of acting." In Rochester she screened films over and over, mostly thanks to George Paatt, who was Jim Card's assistant. Then on July 14, 1964 she voiced this opinion of her work: "Thirty years ago I allowed the critics to break my heart, saying I did not 'act'...I did not do anything, because I did not mug in the conventions of the period. If I am now 'ageless,' it is because I found such antics ludicrous, without beauty, and played all my parts as ballets."

Along with her handful of incandescent performances, her sharp, superb descriptions of her days as a "star" have now gained much praise. I watched her growing as a writer and was privileged, at times, to play editor. Like a careful sculptor, chisel in hand, she picked at the marble until the inner Truth got exposed. Louise Brooks may have been a fearful sinner, but onscreen she left a special legacy. At the end she realized what had happened. "The fire of success burned out in me years ago," she told me in 1968.

About that time, I, "Junior," got replaced in her affections by none other than Roddy McDowall. He had come to Rochester to photograph her, and together with publicist John Springer, bought her for $300 a color TV. My budget didn't allow such lavish gifts, not when my stove was a hot-plate.

Yet each moment I was with her remains clear as crystal. For instance, in 1960, I helped present some programs called "The Movie Star." Louise arrived in New York without Jim Card and I took her to the Hotel Lexington; the programs were held at the Hebrew "Y" at 92nd and Lexington Avenue. When the Lillian Gish film (*The Wind*) was shown, Miss Gish appeared and spoke. Joan Crawford introduced her film—admittedly one she didn't like, *Rain* from 1932; Greta Garbo to nobody's surprise did not come with her film, whose title, alas, I have forgotten. Louise's film was *Prix de Beauté*. Now I had a problem—how to keep her sober until the evening performance?

Through the years, the caps on her teeth had broken off; eventually, Louise herself paid for new ones at the cost of $1500. She was, understandably, self-conscious talking in public.

Lillian Gish, circa 1942

My solution was to buy her a large bouquet of red roses and have her hold them in front of her, rather like the tiger peering through jungle foliage in the painting by Henri Rousseau. Meanwhile, we had the whole day to get through. Inspired, I made arrangements with Lillian Gish to lunch at her near-Victorian flat in the City. For a long time Louise and Lillian had hoped to get together, so Louise was pleased.

As I remember, lunch was Boston baked beans and a molasses-flavored brown bread. Unfortunately, a carafe of wine sat within reach of Brooks. The phone kept ringing and Miss Geesh (as D.W. Griffith called her) on light footsteps vanished to answer calls from MoMA or from John Huston's office. With each call, Louise growled, reaching to pour herself a new glass of wine. Soon she was blotto.

When the wonderful lunch was finished, Miss Gish graciously followed us out to the hall; she wore a delicate silk peignoir. Louise leaned against the wall, grumbling, "Goddamit!" That was too much for Miss Gish. She took hold of Louise's shoulders, shaking them gently.

She declared, "No, Louise. God bless it," and floated back down the hall out of sight.

Many years passed. By an ironic turn of events I had replaced Roddy McDowall on the board of the Gish Film Theater at Bowling Green State University here in Ohio. Once when she visited the theater, I attempted to describe this lunch to Miss Gish. She said in a far-off tone, "You are thinking of my sister Dorothy."

So much for one of the highlights of my life.

However, this is the same Miss Gish who on another occasion informed me that *Broken Blossoms* had to be shot in the

Lillian Gish, circa 1921

middle of the night because Mr. Griffith *had* to accommodate Donald Crisp who was shooting another film in the daytime. This, when Mr. Griffith was the most important director in the business?

Anyway, after the showing at the Hebrew "Y," a number of us, including Adolph Green and Betty Comden and Louise's pal from the *Follies* Peggy Fears and Peggy's chum known as "Miss Fairweather," trooped down to Brooks' old hangout, Glennon's

Quick Comet In the Sky: Louise Brooks

The Gish Theater and Gallery presents
Internationally Acclaimed Author, film historian, and archivist

Jan Wahl
who
——— REMEMBERS ———
Legendary actress

Louise Brooks
(1906-1985)

With a showing of Pandora's Box (1926) and with piano
accompaniment by Stuart Oderman

The Gish Film Theater & Gallery,
Hanna Hall
Bowling Green State University
Bowling Green, Ohio

Sunday, October 12, 1997, at 3:00 p.m.

Bar, on Third Avenue. Jimmy Glennon had torn out the page from *Vanity Fair* with the striking portrait by Steichen. The page hung over the bar in a small black frame. This was my first glimpse of it and I oh'd and ah'd and at that moment "Miss Fairweather" threw up over her brand-new chinchilla.

What if Louise had come to the Warners lot and did *The Public Enemy?* Would her career have flourished? *What if* ...

What if Garbo had done *Madame Curie?*

For that matter, what if Norma Shearer had done *Mrs. Miniver?* If George Raft had not turned down *High Sierra?* What then?

What if, only suppose, Louise *had* done the dialog scenes for *The Canary Murder Case?*

If Louise Brooks were able to play her life over again from the beginning—would she have changed any of it? She was a quick comet in the Hollywood sky. But justice was done and she found her immortality.

I remember so clearly that marvelous voice, fed mostly on memories, gin and a few oyster crackers. I wish most of all that at the end she found peace and wisdom. Truly—my life would have had a hole in it if I had not met her, I am sure of that.

Louise passed away from emphysema and heart failure on August 8, 1985, age seventy-eight. R.I.P., dear friend.

Chapter 8
Comic Strips Were a Fine Art

Somewhere, I saw a simple drawing by Rembrandt—not much more than a line drawn across an otherwise blank page—called "Winter Landscape." The magic was you could feel in your bones the bleak sky above, the coldness of the ground below. All with a hand-drawn line. No machine or robot can equal such genius.

From my point of view, there are no giants today in the arts. No Bach. No Gershwin. No Nijinsky. No Astaire. No Rembrandt. No Parrish. No Caruso. No Crosby. Get my drift? It's intermission time.

What do we have now to fill the void? Rap or computer animation. Can you be content when you review the richness of Not-Long-Ago? What happened?

Once upon a time, there were giants making an American contribution to the arts, to a wonderful original, *the comic strip*. I am crossing my fingers that large museums, even mine in sleepy Toledo, I hope may at last catch up and realize—while they loudly laud Warhol, Lichtenstein or Jim Dine—they neglect this outstanding graphic form. And it was there every day, in everybody's hands: the common newspaper.

Lyonel Feiniger and *The Kin-Der-Kids* (1906) for *Chicago Sunday Tribune*

Comic Strips Were a Fine Art 117

A big clue that art critics glide over is that one of the greatest international artists of last century, Lyonel Feiniger (actually born in Brooklyn), immediately saw the possibilities.

This, in 1906 the *Chicago Tribune* was astute enough to hire him to do a full-color Sunday page which he called *The Kin-der-Kids*. They set out in the family bathtub, these kids—Daniel Webster and Gussie and Pie-Mouth and Strenuous Teddy and Little Japansky, with Uncle Kin-der and Aunt Jim-Jam and the red-haired Pillsbury family. Off they sailed across the Atlantic for weekly adventures.

Here, Feiniger was no less inspired than in his drawings, painting, woodcarvings. He did not see this as a lesser expression. Every week, in six to eight panels, Feiniger never drew "down" and maybe this is why, all too soon, he was persuaded to drop the *Kids* and start another strip which he called *Wee Willie Winkie's*

Feiniger:
Wee Willie Winkie

McCay:
Little Nemo

118 Through a Lens Darkly

Winsor McCay: *Little Nemo*, 1907

World. After several weeks, he was given instead of full color just two colors; black with light green, or black with yellow or orange.

Wee Willie, too, was a fascinating strip: ships had eyes, so did trees and houses. And those Feiniger trains! His haunted, humanized trains intrigued him to the end of his life, particularly in his magic woodcarvings.

Hooray, also in that first decade was a great full Sunday page, a strip better remembered than *Wee Willie* or the *Kids*.

It was Winsor McCay's *Little Nemo in Slumberland*. Whereas Feiniger worked in expressionistic style, cone-shaped bodies, elongated forms, trees stretched as far as a large panel could accommodate, Winsor McCay was knee-deep in a delicate art nouveau mode. Each Sunday, Nemo had a lyrical nightmare with odd characters whom he met in his elaborate dream. Maurice Sendak's picture book, *In the Night Kitchen*, is a tribute to the superior McCay.

Interestingly enough, Winsor McCay was a pioneer of animation. In fact, he began animating *Little Nemo* as early as 1911. Some of the prints were hand-colored. This incredibly fluid short is superior to the more famous *Gertie the Dinosaur* that some books list as his first cartoon. Not so. Both, however, are landmarks in the genre.

Not surprisingly, movies and comic strips share fundamental qualities from their very beginning.

Each medium tells its story in a given set of frames or images. You can argue the comic strip was inspired by the motion picture. Both are entertainments that soon grew into an art. In the comics, it's all laid out there on the page. The eye and imagination make the movement.

Also, interestingly enough, the best early movies and Sunday comic strips relied a lot on high fantasy. The first giant of filmmakers was a Frenchman, Georges Méliès, a magician from the Theatre Robert Houdin.

George Herriman: *Krazy Kat*, 1937

Over one hundred years ago, in his trick-films, *Cinderella* and *A Trip to the Moon*, he used those special properties of film, such as stop-motion and superimposition, to tell his fairy stories and science fiction. Many prints of works by Méliès were also meticulously hand-painted. Deliriously beautiful.

Both the movies and the comic strips are unique graphic forms. It's a mistake to pigeonhole movies as simply an extended form of photography. The careful, laborious hand-coloring of each frame of film was very much like the glorious bright colors added by the inks of the printer.

In the initial quarter century or so, comics were respected by the syndicates and were published with warm pride. This is evident by the amount of space they were given; plenty of room to draw in, and they inhabited a world of their own.

Now look at today's newspapers, with the space given *The Wizard of Id*, *Garfield*, *Baby Blues* and *Cathy*. Smaller art, smaller talents. At least *Beetle Bailey* has memorable characters, Sarge, Beetle, General Halftrack, Miss Buxley.

The last strip I would call genuine art is Bill Watterson's delectable *Calvin and Hobbes*, in which a kid has the notion his toy tiger has a life of its own. Delusion or imagination? I call it the latter, especially whenever Calvin goes into outer space or meets (very gorgeously drawn) dinosaurs. On Sundays, when *Calvin* was introduced, Watterson was given his own whole page. Later he got only half a page. Ultimately he was told he'd have but a third of a Sunday page. Time to quit. A wise decision. Our loss. Calvin lives on in books.

To return to the heyday of the past century when Lively Arts were indeed lively, not mere recycled ideas of their betters,

Comic Strips Were a Fine Art 121

George Herriman: *Krazy Kat*, circa 1934

Cliff Sterrett: *Paw Perkins*, circa 1935

soon after *Nemo* came what some feel was the best of the best. The delightfully zany strip *Krazy Kat* by George Herriman.

The Kat was a he. Or maybe a she. Krazy was like the androgynous member of Hal Roach's two-reel silent comedies *Our Gang*, Farina. (Farina, with cornrows and oversized shoes, and roly-poly doll Little Joe Cobb, are nifty visual characters.)

Krazy Kat inhabited a far realm suggesting the South-West but where a moon may happen to change shape in a single night and where Ignatz Mouse, apparently married, often to relieve himself of tensions at home, was wont to bean Kat with a tossed brick. Invariably, Ignatz is jailed by Offisa Pup. Krazy took the conk on the noggin mistakenly as proof of Ignatz's affection.

Sterret: *Polly and Her Pals*, circa 1935

No matter what you might say about William Randolph Hearst (and plenty has been said, with good reason), he kept *Krazy Kat* going for decades after most papers dropped it.

This marvelous, one-of-a-kind strip was not well served by the animators hoping to equal its originality. Gregory La Cava, the future director of *My Man Godfrey*, worked on a series in 1916. A decade later, producer Charles Mintz (Disney's nemesis) revived *Kat*, continuing well into the Thirties at Columbia. On occasion, one of the Columbias was A-1. *The Crystal Gazebo* of 1932, is a good cartoon but no Herriman. Not up to par.

As much as any human ever did, George Herriman understood surrealism. To boot, he was gifted with a literary style of his own.

There was one other stupendous strip, called *Polly and Her Pals*. This strip, less known but no less magnificent, was by Cliff Sterrett. Miracle of miracles, *Polly* also had a long, long life, longer than *Nemo*, *The Kin-der-Kids* or *Krazy*. Who the guardian angel was keeping *Polly* alive, I don't know. As did Feiniger, McCay or Herriman, Cliff Sterrett borrowed from no one. He created his own thing.

And what a thing! Polly's family consisted of her parents, Maw and Paw Perkins, the darndest-looking cat you ever saw, and several obnoxious relations who never stopped invading the household: snooty Carrie and her brat Gertrude, plus that rascal nephew Ashur.

Only one person truly understood bumbling, lovable, scatterbrain Paw. Who? The Japanese houseboy, Neewah. Indeed, *Polly and Her Pals* was really about Paw and not Polly herself.

To tell the truth, in its finest moments, it needed no words whatsoever. Just that sublime, goofy drawing, with bright flat jolly colors each Sunday, stylized rows of houses with peaked roofs, hilarious flowers and occasional bunnies, the black sky and round moon, all made this strip oddly memorable.

Unbelievably, *Polly* lasted forty-six years! Toward the end, when for physical reasons Cliff Sterrett was not up to it, the daily strip was ghosted by another brilliant artist, Paul Fung.

The strips I've mentioned, with this exception, were drawn and written by their creators exclusively. Ditto some other swell ones, including *Popeye* by Elie Segar. (When Segar died in an accident, other artists kept the strip going, if not with the same gusto and inventiveness.) *Skippy* by Percy Crosby. *Dick Tracy* by Chester Gould. *Little Orphan Annie* by Harold Gray. *Barnaby* by Crockett Johnson.

All these, save *Barnaby*, became movies of various kinds—animated, musical. The most faithful to the original was Max Fleischer's animated *Popeye*. In fact he made a wonderful contribution: Popeye regains his strength by eating spinach, which most kids loathe. He made it popular.

A famous Peter Arno cartoon in *The New Yorker* has a Park Avenue child scowling at her plate. "I say it's spinach—and I say to hell with it!"

The big live-action movies of *Dick Tracy* and *Popeye* don't make the grade. Tess Trueheart and Junior are fine; Warren Beatty is no Dick Tracy. They get Olive Oyl right on target, but Robin Williams is no more Popeye than I am.

Movies and comic strips have this in common: they are *archives of their own time*. Earlier in the 20th Century, you sense an art inventing itself. After the giddiness that energized the Twenties fell to Earth with a grand plop, in the Depression Thirties comics grew serious, with many of them becoming soap operas. The words were more important than the pictures. Almost always.

Much later, there's a sloppy charm to *Pogo* and *Peanuts*. Yet they are just not in the same league as the art of *Polly*. The humor in them is more in the words, not pictures.

Look for yourself. You can enjoy the glorious antics of the *Kids*, *Nemo*, *Krazy* and *Polly* in handsome editions put out by Kitchen Sink Press.

The comic artists I am fondest of—Herriman, Feiniger, Sterrett and McCay—without a doubt are proprietors of their own universe. Each with a special style and a special authority.

We will not see their likes again.

Winsor McCay: *Little Nemo*, circa 1908

Chapter 9

Butterflies Across the Meadow:
Ernest Thesiger, Ruth St. Denis and Paul Swan

Question: When must a circus performer quit? Answer: Before he or she falls off a tight wire. But for many performers, it's hard to guess.

Now when I lived in Mexico, in the state of Guanajuato, it happened to be my birthday and Bing Crosby came to town to play golf. He was told it was my natal day and across the table he warbled a few flawless bars of "Happy Birthday." What a glorious moment—fantastic! Der Bingle singing to me!

The astonishing thing is the voice was in super shape, no surprise to me since earlier in the year I had seen him on American TV with Bette Midler. They were playful together; the program was impressive proof that someone in his late seventies, as Mr. Crosby was, defied time itself.

Alas—it was at the close of that show that, when he leaned down from the stage to greet well-wishers, he toppled off into the music pit which had been lowered—a fall of thirty feet.

Crosby died in Spain that year (playing golf). Surely, the fall hastened his demise. But he was still Der Bingle, the greatest of

Ernest Thesinger (1935)   (Sig Humanski Collection)

all popular vocalists, when he sat across the table and belted out "Happy Birthday." Other performers perform past their prime, yet the urge to keep doing it is strong.

It's been my privilege to meet a number of these extraordinary people just before they croaked. I mean, it's a privilege to meet them, simply to be in close proximity to somebody who is legendary. A case in point: I was in London once and bumped into James Broughton, the San Francisco avant-garde filmmaker of *Pleasure Garden*, *Mother's Day* and *Loony Tom the Happy Lover*.

Jim mentioned he was about to have tea up at Ivy Compton Burnett's, the novelist of books that equal the wit of Wilde himself, all entirely told in dialog, real *tour de forces*. What a conversationalist she must be! He asked if I wanted to come along. I was burning to go and traipsed after him.

Paul Swan (1915)

Paul Swan by Arnold Genthe (1921)

I remember the ancient lady had her hair in a snood; her flat was three flights up. As it happened, this person whom I figured must be a fabulous raconteuse only opened her mouth once or twice. She was a listener, not a talker. A number of us sat cozily around, stirring sugar in our tea quietly, waiting for Ivy Compton Burnett to regale us with her wit and charm when the door opened.

In hobbled a gentleman who seemed to be one hundred years old. Or more. It was none other than Ernest Thesiger, the wizened Dr. Pretorious of James Whale's *Bride of Frankenstein*, the eccentric Horace Femm ("Do have a potato!") of Whale's *The Old Dark House*. He gasped for breath, apparently a victim of acute asthma. The climb up the stairs had been too much. He held in fluttering pale bony fingers boxes of scones, his contribu-

Ruth St. Denis and husband Ted Shawn (1922)

tion to the tea party. He was too weak to untangle the strings that held the little white boxes together. His panting was alarming. It lasted for many minutes. At last, Ivy Compton Burnett spoke.

"That pansy!" she sneered in her superior aristocratic manner. To tell the truth, I wanted to kneel at his feet. I adored him in the Whale horror classics. I couldn't believe it—I'm sitting in the same room with Dr. Pretorious. *He's alive!*

Still at age eighty the grand old man was acting, he had a couple of major films ahead. He had just finished *The Horse's Mouth* and soon was to do *Sons and Lovers* and *The Roman Spring of Mrs. Stone*. A remarkable man. But the asthma was alarming.

A last word about the scones-toting, enigmatic Ernest Thesiger: his fellow soldiers during WWI were in awe of him when, in the front lines, horrors raging everywhere, he sat calmly in the trenches doing what he liked best—elegant needlepoint.

One story I want to tell is about Paul Swan, who was once known as "The World's Most Beautiful Man." That was in 1915. I got to know him about fifty years later. I was in my twenties. He gave surreal Sunday afternoon programs in his huge, eerie studio at Carnegie Hall, where he attracted unusual attendees—either very, *very* old ladies who had swooned over him in their youth, or very, *very* young men who were painted and powdered as much as he was.

Let me digress.

Several years later, also in the Big Apple, legendary Ruth St. Denis was to have a matinee appearance at Columbia University. I rushed off. Am I really going to see Ruth St. Denis dance? Can it be true? What was she—a hundred years old?

Ruth St. Denis in her "Kwannon" dance
by Baron Adolph de Meyer (1922)

There was to be The Dance of the Golden Madonna, followed by The Dance of the Silver Madonna. The pianist played a blending of Debussy and Ravel. Curtains parted. It was she, the historical personage who'd danced in the Babylonian sequence of D.W. Griffith's *Intolerance* in 1916. The stately Miss St. Denis wore a floor-length gold lamé gown. She stood like a statue, holding before her a golden platter.

The piano continued. She didn't move. Until I noticed, yes, her feet were not moving; however, in time to the accompaniment, she moved the platter from side to side.

It moved…slowly…so slowly…ever so slowly. The plate was dancing! At last the curtains closed for a tantalizingly long while, then opened again. Now Miss Denis was dressed in a silver lame gown and she held a platter of shiny silver, doing you guess it. The Dance of the Silver Madonna. Unforgettable. I was actually witnessing Ruth St. Denis *moving*.

And back to "The World's Most Beautiful Man," who once had appeared in a two-reel "art" dance film in tinted colors: *Diana the Huntress*, underwritten by the Baroness Von De Witz, who took the part of Diana. Paul Swan was her brother, Apollo. In the cast were Florence Fleming Noyes and Her Dancing Pupils.

There was an awful lot of frantic rapturous leapings about, flailing of arms and floating silk scarves. There were special effects: the Sun God Apollo racing through clouds, and Diana forlorn on the Moon, where she shoots her arrows back to Earth. The arrows turn into flowers that are gathered by Acteon. It's all very lyrical. Acteon is transformed into a stag and gets shot by his own hunters. Diana awakens sleeping Endymion and all ends happily.

My favorite scene: the Bubble Dance at the enchanted pool. To tell the truth, both Pan and Endymion are better looking than The World's Most Beautiful Man. It doesn't matter. Paul Swan, painted with layers of make-up, as he continued to do for the next half century, remained comfortable in a time warp of his own. Pavlova and Nijinsky and Balanchine never happened. The time warp was evident in his mysterious Carnegie Hall studio, hung with velvet drapes and huge paintings in classic poses, himself imagined by himself. His dance recitals, as a very old man, were something to behold.

My friend, the painter Robert Barnes, often attended, as did Andy Warhol and Marcel Duchamp. I was loathe to miss these Sunday recitals. No matter what some members of the audience might think privately, everyone remained respectful. After all, there was only one Paul Swan.

He invited me to go to meetings of occult societies, so we walked through the city streets at night probably like two vampires—one an elderly, heavily-painted person wearing a large black hat and a flowing black cape, and by his side a nervous young fellow trotting along. And I attended his final performance.

Somehow he got through Butterflies Across the Meadow. Then he hid behind the draperies to catch his breath. Next he rolled out a giant papier-mâché Sphinx which he had constructed. He wore only a kind of girdle of tin can lids strung about his waist. His skin was stark white, and made the kohl about his eyes more intense. He danced The Bacchanal of the Sahara Desert with much abandon. At the close, which much effort, he climbed atop the Sphinx and leaped off.

PAUL SWAN
THE CELEBRATED MIME - DANSEUR
RECITALS
EVERY SUNDAY EVENING, at 8:30
MISS EVELYN HANSEN
PIANIST

"Paul Swan gave his weekly program of original dance interpretations last evening in his Carnegie Hall studio.

That statement only mildly indicates the wonderful quality of his art, the deep sensitivity of his revelations, and the rare mentality that prompts his performance and the versatility of his achievements.
GRENA BENNETT, New York (Journal-American):

19,378 *Persons Have Attended These Unique Recitals*

SEE, "WHO'S WHO IN AMERICA"

CARNEGIE HALL, STUDIO 90.
154 WEST 57th STREET   Tel. Circle 6-7082

As he jumped, he grabbed his loins, giving a yelp—he had a hernia. He hobbled off in pain, followed by some old ladies and young men who tried to console him. It was a stunner. The following week a short notice in *The Times* declared, owing to circumstances, Paul Swan was discontinuing his incredible Sunday recitals.

What Paul Swan is remembered for today is his art—not the fleeting ethereal art of the dance, not for his movie: it's for his remarkable drawings and paintings and sculpture. In Paris he was

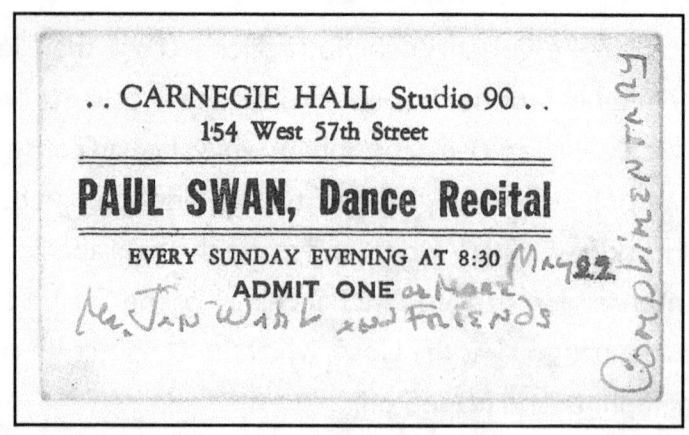

..CARNEGIE HALL Studio 90..
154 West 57th Street
PAUL SWAN, Dance Recital
EVERY SUNDAY EVENING AT 8:30
ADMIT ONE

Pencil portrait of Jan Wahl by Paul Swan

equally famous for them in his lifetime. His sculpture, perhaps not quite on the same high shelf as Rodin, is near the quality of Antoine Bourdelle. It is timeless, inspired by long-ago Greeks. And is his legacy supreme. Paul Swan sought to conquer time itself. Maybe he did, in one way or another.

I salute Paul Swan, Ruth St. Denis. In memory, they are ever youthful, ever nimble, fantastical.

Historical Footnote: Let me add that Paul Swan is immortalized in Cecil B. DeMille's 1923 extravaganza *The Ten Commandments* as Captain of the Pharaoh's Guard. Inexplicably he went under the name "John Randolph." However he believed he was, by participating in a major film, on his way to "universal glory."

Chapter 10
A Cup of Coffee for Carl Th. Dreyer

Once upon a time, to be more exact, a half century ago and more, I sailed on a Norwegian liner, the stately *Oslofjord*, bound for the fairytale country of Denmark, to attend the University of Copenhagen. I say fairytale country because it was then a place where wishes come true.

We were eight days at sea: blissful experience even when a terrible storm struck midway on our journey, the ocean liner rocked to and fro. It was blissful because of the company I kept onboard—young, carefree Scandinavians in the tourist class, mostly Norwegians and Swedes all returning home after a year or at least a summer in the United States.

Hearts were light. Many were students; I bunked with two lieutenants in the Norwegian Air Force. Often there were dances on deck with lots of music, Scandinavian folk tunes and folksongs; and need I add, incredible food. All new to me.

When the storm hit we found it a comic interlude. During the night it was like lying in the biggest cradle in the world, rocking wildly to and fro. Clink, clatter and crash of breaking crockery made our meals livelier. The height of surreal hilarity was when our waiters, attempting to navigate the slope of the floor, dropped food platters; best of all was when the pianist in the lounge threw up over his piano keys. It was that time of life when, no matter what, things seem lyrical and part of a never-ending game.

Nothing could dampen our high spirits. We were floating without care between two continents. Life was forever!

At last, on the eighth morning, we reached the deep fjords of Norway. It was sun-up, the air was fresh, and all classes were allowed to mingle. Passengers walked anywhere on the ship to enjoy the staggeringly magnificent scenery from any angle we desired. Wisps of early morning smoke curled upward from cottage roofs high on the steep mountains.

A family from Texas was pressed against the rail, studying this spectacle. All six of them wore immaculate white leather boots and matching 10-gallon hats; the father stared and stared; none of them muttering a word. Finally, he felt compelled to say something.

"Nice!" was his observation.

And that was it.

Soon as we reached port, Norwegians rushed down the gangplank. The rest of us left the land of trolls and goat cheese. That cheese rather resembles and tastes like brown laundry soap—not displeasing once you get used to it.

And the Oslofjord steered straight into the Copenhagen harbor, past Den Lille Havfrue (The Little Mermaid), dreaming on her rock at Langelinie. This was Hans Christian Andersen country. Waiting on the dock was Fru Jensen from the Scandinavian-American Foundation.

She waved a tall banner with very bold letters: WELCOME JAN WAHL. As if I were some arriving celebrity and not a greenhorn from Toledo.

Fru Jensen found me a room with a balcony at the large flat of a well-known painter of Greenland landscape and Eskimos, Oda Isbrand (Isbrand = Ice Fire) on Gothersgade, across from Rosenborg Castle with its park and moat where swans lazily glided. From my window I saw the Round Tower up which Peter the Great once rode with his coach and horses. Instantly, I knew I was in an enchanted spot.

For this was the land of H.C. Andersen (no Dane refers to him as Hans Christian) and Tuborg and Carlsberg beers, and open-face sandwiches (works of art in themselves), the Tivoli Gardens with its fireworks and, exciting me the most, this is where my favorite living writer lived, Isak Dinesen, known to Danes as the Baroness Karen Blixen-Finecke, author of *Seven Gothic Tales* and *Out of Africa*. And to top that, this was the home of my favorite living moviemaker, Carl Theodor Dreyer, whose *La Passion de Jeanne d'Arc* from 1928 I thought was the towering achievement of cinema; his only rival to me was F. W. Murnau with *Sunrise* from 1927. Perhaps I may be a purist and a snob, but to me silent films are the pinnacles of movie art.

At once it was arranged that my adviser was to be Erik Saxtorph, a specialist in Danish film history as well as Danish folklore. I was in double heaven.

Copenhagen is a city made for strolling and I often walked down Gothersgade toward the Opera House, Kongens Nytor and Nyhavn and the harbor. I'd pass by a shop with shabby small pleasures and always, no matter the weather, the owner hung on a peg over the entrance a modest-sized oil painting which I believed to be a French landscape. It was covered with years of neglect. On day, I crossed the street to inquire its price. In kroner (crowns) it amounted to about eight dollars. "Too much!" I said. "Needs lots of cleaning."

It caught my eye nevertheless on days fair or foul, until one morning it was gone. The peg was empty. On the front page of the newspapers read a headline: "LOST GAUGHIN FOUND." Of course you know Paul Gaughin married a shrewish Danish wife, worked at a dreary bank until he escaped from wife, children and job, to live on the sunny isle of Tahiti. For $8 I might have had me a real Gaughin.

One noon I was at the Town Hall Square which bustled with activity. People bought flowers or the daily *Extrabladet* or were enjoying the tasty pølser. That is until a German family, Mama, Papa and two kids, popped out from a Mercedes and ran across the square.

The father, in triumph, shouted, "There! There was my office!" Oh my. Every Dane knew that building at which he was pointing, the Shell Oil House, had been the Nazi Administration Headquarters during the war. No one else spoke. The crowd simply shunned them, literally turning their backs on them. Silence was deafening.

Germans were not allowed as tourists in Denmark until years after the war. Because Demark was part of NATO, eventually they made their way north again. Another time I visited a friend's aunt and uncle up in Norway; they lived in a handsome manor house that the Nazis had seized, billeting officers there, the aunt and uncle being servants to the Germans in their own house. While we were at lunch, a maid came in to inform my hosts there were visitors. The gentleman wished to show his wife where he had spent several happy years.

Carl Th. Dreyer at the time he made *Day of Wrath* (1943)

"They were *not* happy years," replied Herr Gad. "Send them away."

Copenhagen is a splendid city for walking; you are always within a couple of blocks from a lovely park. The streets in the center are crooked, not straight, since, centuries earlier, the British had set fire to the city; it had to be rebuilt. The King said he never again wished to look down a street to see an Englishman at the end of it.

Anyway, while wandering one spring afternoon, I was stopped by Broderick Crawford who wore a rumbled American raincoat. "Hey, kid—you speak the English?" In some kind of makeshift accent I allowed I spoke "a little bit." Broderick Crawford—who played Lennie on Broadway in Steinbeck's *Of Mice and Men*, who was terrific in the Damon Runyan comedy *Tight Shoes*—Broderick Crawford of *All the King's Men* and *Born Yesterday*. Could I help him?

He told me he heard Copenhagen had silver shops with old English silver. Would I guide him to one? Sure I would. Now my problem was I had answered in a fake accent. So I confused the shopkeeper. What country was I from? But I kept it up and bargained for excellent low prices. He offered to purchase for me a thank-you gift. I chose an English coffee urn from around 1800, wonderfully modern in design.

"Your English is pretty good," he said. "You could pass for an American." I thanked him for the compliment and walked Mr. Crawford back to his hotel which happened to the Angleterre at Kongens Nytorv. In my improvised accent I informed him Danes did not like to stay there.

"Why, kid?" he asked. "Because," I informed him, "the Angleterre was home to high-ranking Nazi brass during the war."

"Hell, I'm checking out!" he growled—rushing up to the front desk. Quickly, I melted away into a rainy afternoon.

My birthday is in April, so were the ones of King Frederick and Queen Ingrid. The wife of a newspaper publisher got me invited as an "American poet" to their shared fødseldag celebra-

Broderick Crawford, circa 1952

tion. Off I went to Amalienborg, where I hobnobbed with the Prime Minister, a symphony conductor, poets and singers. My first taste of schnapps. Ice-cold danger. Exhilarating if followed by a beer chaser.

After a couple of them, I was feeling bold. When it was my turn to shake the King's hand, I asked him a question swimming in my brain: was it true, when he served in the Royal Navy, he had

Carl Th. Dreyer: *Vampyr* (1932)

a chrysanthemum tattooed on his back in Tokyo? I detected a twinkle in his eye and he guided me out of the room, removed his black silk jacket and his shirt. There it was—magnificent art. Incredible! Not only that, after we returned, he handed me the antique schnapps glass he drank from; a real treasure.

Call it chutzpah of youth, or too much schnapps. When I giddily described my evening out with my landlady, Fru Isbrand, she wondered why I wasn't removed from the premises. As for me, I got a royal memento and thought King Frederick pretty neat.

Then, in the papers, it said my hero, Carl Theodor Dreyer, who made *La Passion de Jeanne d'Arc* and *Vampyr*, was about to direct a new film. I guess it was time to let him know I was in town. I must have written Herr Dreyer a decent letter because he wrote back suggesting I travel up to Rungsted, where he and his wife Ebba were renting a small villa. Rungsted—the same place where Isak Dinesen lived! The stars shone down on me.

At Rungsted, despite my numbness in the presence of the master director, he made every effort to put me at ease. He was surprised I knew about Kaj Munk who wrote the play on which *Ordet* ("The Word") was to be based. Dreyer outlined the story as we briskly strolled along.

I must have passed his test, because after my exams I got a postcard inviting me to participate in the making of *Ordet*, the new project. Denmark was a magic land. All doors opened to a student masquerading as a poet.

Kaj Munk, the pastor who wrote the play, became a symbol of Denmark resistance when he was murdered by Nazis for being too outspoken. His story was about a theological student named Johannes who studies too intently, cracks up and assumes *he*

Deleted scene from *Vampyr*. Dreyer decided not to use the wolf motif (Gift from Dreyer)

must be Jesus the Christ. Its setting is the west coast of Jutland where life is hardest and a living must be made both from land and sea, farming and fishing. These people are strong believers who, after Sunday church, meet at each other's houses drinking strong coffee and discussing the morning's sermon.

This explains the advertising slogan that reads, with Danish wit: "*There Is No Spiritual Life Without Cirkel Coffee.*"

Ordet is laid in 1925 or thereabouts. The story deals with opposing Christian sects, practiced by two families; one, led by old Morten Borgen the farmer, known as the kindly ones. Johannes is the second son. The other family is that of Peter the Tailor, leading a group known as the sour-faced ones. There's a Romeo and Juliet-type romance between the old farmer's third son and the daughter of the tailor.

Most importantly, *Ordet* deals with a miracle. Inger, wife to Morten Borgen's oldest son, dies in childbirth; when mad Johannes returns to sanity, he is able to raise his beloved sister-in-law from the dead as she lies in her coffin. A question of belief, love and faith. Not easy to tackle.

Strong stuff, a project like this that ends in a miracle.

Herr Dreyer told me that this was an in-between project—sort of preparation for his vast Jesus-film, the one he wished to do more than any other. But that summer of 1954 was drizzly and cloudy. What was meant to be a two-week location shoot, took most of the summer. Nevertheless, Dreyer remained calm, spoke softly, so the atmosphere was one almost of meditation, one of intense quiet. Once or twice there were problems with the cameraman, Henning Bendtsen, who had his own ideas. I believe his young assistant, John Carlsen, was more in tune with what Dreyer wanted.

Resurrection scene from *Ordet* with Cay Kristiansen, Brigitte Federspiel and Henrik Malberg

I saw enough to convince me not to be a movie director. You must be a field marshal commanding an army of nervous actors, temperamental technicians, all of whom must bend to the will of the person in charge.

A Dreyer film can never, never be mistaken for a film by anybody else.

Dreyer shared what he wanted not by shouting; sometimes in silence. Nothing was rushed. When he did "lose" it, for instance with Henning Bendtsen, he simply took his cup of coffee and walked away.

We waited a full week for the title shot of *Ordet*. The camera was to be pushed (on a track) and panned across the front yard of the farm, "Borgensgaard." A filter on the lens made it appear to be nighttime. There were sheep grazing, clothes hanging on the line. Herr Dreyer wanted the clouds to part in a certain way, letting light shine down, making the grass shiny. Day after day it either rained or clouds did not cooperate.

One afternoon the sky looked gloomy as usual, so I slipped into the house to ask Fru Chrstensen, whose house it was, to cheer us up by making pots and pots of coffee. After Madam Blue (that's the name for the enamel pot) was filled with piping-hot Cirkel coffee, I opened the front door. I called out, "Surprise!"

The surprise was mine, unfortunately—the clouds cooperated just as Dreyer had been hoping for and his camera was moving across the yard, pushed perfectly by the crew. It caught me opening the door. Dreyer's eyes, normally light-blue, went entirely blank. They lost their color.

The same thing happened when the love-struck third son, Anders, went searching for his mad brother Johannes; the young

Jackie Coogan in *The Kid* (1921)

Jackie Coogan as *Peck's Bad Boy* (1923)
Photo by James Abbe

actor, who in real life was a school teacher, was to come out from a sheep shelter, cup his hands, and holler, "Johannes! Johannes!" This had been practiced a number of times—the camera moving just so. At last all elements were perfect. The young man came out of the shelter, cupped his hands, and he cried: "*Anders! Anders!*" He was yelling his own name.

Dreyer's eyes lost their color.

Herr Kristensen (the farm's owner), Erik Aaes (studio set designer) and Dreyer on location for *Ordet*

Preben Lerdorff Rye as Johannes, Dreyer with camera crew and young visitor on location for *Ordet*

Carl Th. Dreyer (at left), Jan Wahl (black sweater), Karen Petersen (script-girl) and actors on lunch break: *Ordet*

A Cup of Coffee for Carl Th. Dreyer

An odd event happened before we departed for Jutland. A large shiny cranium popped into a doorway at Palladium. "Hi there, I'm Jackie!" the head bellowed. This very big person had been *The Kid* (with Chaplin), *Oliver Twist* (with Lon Chaney) and *Peck's Bad Boy*. No vestige of what he once had been, save for an innocent enthusiasm.

Turns out he had a bright idea for a feature film: he'd play a CIA agent chasing Russian spies through Copenhagen's pleasure park, Tivoli. His inspiration was to utilize the roller-coaster and spectacular fireworks display. It must be in color!

Palladium bosses were entranced. Here's an American super superstar. Jackie Coogan! This would be Denmark's first Eastmancolor project. Important things first! Palladium's most up-to-date camera got whisked away from Dreyer for a movie so awful it was never released.

And so one camera (of the two) Dreyer had at his disposal on the location shoot was a rickety silent Debrie. The soundtrack would be added later at the studio. Rather like the way the master filmed *Vampyr* in France in 1932.

(My friend David Shepard at Blackhawk Films told me that when *Oliver Twist* was restored in the early 1970s with the aid of Jackie Coogan and Sol Lesser, its original producer, Jackie had an incredible recollection of exact wording of the titles, since a 35mm long-lost print, minus intertitles, had surfaced in Yugoslavia. The child star may have less charm and sparkle than he had years before, but his memory was sharp.)

The great man needed a 1925 farming newspaper; not one to be read but in case the actors happened to pick it up where it was to lie on the set when we went to Palladium Studios. It must be the correct vintage. So I got on my bicycle and rode practically the length of Jutland, stopping everywhere until I found one thirty years old in mint condition.

An example of Dreyer the perfectionist.

Throughout the summer I was privileged to sit always at Dreyer's left at the table; we had wonderful conversations. That

Asta Nielsen, circa 1917

Asta Nielsen and reporter with two of her cloth collages (1951)

is, I listened spellbound. Dreyer was a visionary—he was there and not there, so intense was his concentration. If he looked at the script, it was in the privacy of his room at the hotel.

Dreyer did not wish to talk about past works, but rather to think ahead on future projects. His *Medea*-film, his *Mary Stuart*-film, his *Jesus*-film. All living in his head. The scripts were done; he never won the means to see them through, but a full ten years following completion of *Ordet* he did direct *Gertrud*. Never having the chance to work in color, he had inspiring color theories.

For instance, he said why can't grass be blue, as in impressionist paintings. If it suits the mood?

When we finished at Vedersø, in Jutland, we returned to Copenhagen where the interiors, designed by Erik Aaes, who'd done the sets for *The Day of Wrath* a decade earlier, were waiting.

Asta Nielsen in *The Joyless Street* (1925)

A Cup of Coffee for Carl Th. Dreyer

I watched as Dreyer carefully, thoughtfully removed pots, pans, ladles which hung on hooks on the kitchen walls until he left only a few pieces, just enough to suggest "kitchen." A kitchen which also had running water in the sink, although it was never used. If you pulled out a drawer, utensils were lying there. He did not want the actors to be cheated.

Many nights I was invited to the Dreyer flat in Frederiksberg at number 81 Dalgas Boulevard—a stone's throw from where Asta Nielsen, Denmark's legend, resided. As a treat, he gave me a cigar I swear was a foot long, from Cuba. I was not a smoker and almost died on the spot while we went over the *Medea* pages.

We puffed away on our cigars and the great man asked me whom I could see as Medea. I had two immediate nominations: if for wider appeal, what about Sophia Loren. More "artistic," I nominated Maria Callas. And through the Paramount office in Paris we sent copies of the script to both ladies. Neither replied, I regret to report.

Two ironies: about a year later, my mother showed me an interview in *Ladies Home Journal* or *Women's Home Companion*, I don't recall which. It was with Sophia Loren, who said all her life she'd been burning to portray the character Medea. Hmm. But the director who ultimately made *Medea* was Pasolini in 1970. With guess whom? Callas. Pasolini also jumped the gun on Dreyer, making *The Gospel According to Saint Matthew* in 1964.

I can forgive Pier Paolo Pasolini for one reason only: he made *The Witches* with my favorite Italian beauty, Silvana Mangano, brilliantly playing multiple roles in 1967, the same year he also did *Oedipus Rex*. Pasolini certainly tried big. Perhaps he felt he was paying tribute.

My last evening at the Dreyer flat was an odd one. He had received from a glass-maker in Venice a most fragile all-glass espresso contraption. The Dreyers uncrated the thing from its wooden box, lifting it with respect as if it were the Holy Grail itself from excelsior packing. It gleamed in the lamplight and Carl Theodor Dreyer sat in rapture. It had been a long time in coming. His wife Ebba lit a Bunsen burner, and very, very gradually water bubbled and boiled and after an eternity, drop by drop, black liquid filled the tiny espresso cup. "The first cup is for you, Herr Wahl," he said solemnly. What an honor!

I reached forward to take it from his hand and my right elbow happened to knock the glass machine off the table.

The precious object shattered into a million itty-bitty pieces. Now I had a dilemma. I held the only cup of espresso this machine was ever to emit…What to do. Be the guest, quaff, savor it? Or hand it over to Herr Dreyer, who'd been looking forward to the moment for months?

While I struggled to resolve this, wanting to rewind and this time not bump the darn thing off the table, Dreyer's and his wife's eyes too went blank. I had four Orphan Annie eyes staring.

Memory is merciful—I don't remember the exit from number 81 Dalgas Boulevard.

It seemed prudent that I take my scholarship from the University of Michigan and move on. Ever the kindly one, Dreyer graciously invited me to come to Palladium the week before I left. He was to begin the studio scenes. The end of a blessed summer for which, luckily, I had kept a daily journal. I also had the notes from many of our conversations which, by mail, he diligently corrected, amended and edited in his own precise handwriting.

A pity I couldn't see *Ordet* through to the finish. But often he would close the set so that only camera crew and soundman and actors were there. This would have been the case during the difficult miracle scene of Inger coming back to life.

Ordet is a slow-moving work, yet like many a classic draws the audience into its unique orbit. The camera is a constant bystander—sometimes moving slowly, sometimes patiently observing. No need for rapid cutting or close-ups.

The completed film won many Best of 1955 honors, including Golden Lion at the Venice Film Festival, Golden Globe Award from the Hollywood Press Association and a Danish Oscar, the "Bodil." It got the recognition Dreyer deserved.

Flash forward to 1967. I did not get to know the renowned Asta Nielsen until that summer. The Divine Asta, the Tenth Muse as she was called, was born in 1881. She was the first international movie star—before Charlie Chaplin, or Mary Pickford. Her range was astonishing.

She appeared in a short feature (three reels) in 1910, *Afgrunden* ("The Abyss"). After successful films for Nordisk in Demark, she went to Germany; she made light comedies, she played *Hamlet* in 1920 (somewhat like Garbo in *Queen Christina*, a woman pretending to be a man), she played *Camille* onstage in Berlin, she played in heavy film drama such as *The Tragedy of the Street* opposite Oskar Homolka in 1927. When the Nazis stepped in, she stepped out, returning to Copenhagen, where unfairly her countrymen considered her a German.

Her flat in Frederiksberg was on a grand scale, full of fabulous antiques from her glorious Berlin flat. We drank tea from Sèvres porcelain from the 1700s; she slept in an ornately-carved Spanish bed from the 1600s. While Dreyer eventually got the man-

Asta Nielsen as *Hamlet* (1920)

agership of a movie theater (so did the other great Danish film director, Benjamin Christensen), thus securing a livelihood, this was denied Divine Asta.

By the time I knew her, when she was in her high eighties, she eked out monies by making cloth découpages—elaborate displays of flowers, hens and roosters. Some she kept for herself. Handsomely framed, they looked at home among her baroque paintings and artifacts.

One afternoon we sat at teatime. I asked in my makeshift Danish how it was to have worked with Conrad Veidt in *Der Reigen* in 1920. I had to yell inasmuch as she was hard of hearing.

"Morphinist!" she replied.

Well, let's try Greta Garbo. After all both had been in G.W. Pabst's *The Joyless Street* in 1925.

"Hermaphrodite!" she sniffed.

"Let's talk about you," I said. And as I spoke, I noticed with horror when I lifted up the Sevres cup the dainty saucer stuck to it, because of a sugar paste that wedded them together. When had it been washed last? Then worse, as in slow motion, the priceless saucer fell onto the thick Persian carpet and rolled, over and over and over, the length of the whole room—by a miracle turned a corner, rolling beneath her canopied Spanish bed.

I was stunned. At the beginning frozen in my seat, then I galloped after it as her large orbs grew bigger and bigger in disbelief, in contrast to the Dreyers whose pupils disappeared.

She forgave or she forgot. Anyhow, she made for me a wonderful self-portrait from scraps of fabric—from dresses or silk stockings. I was expecting "Asta Nielsen as Hamlet," as in her remarkable film. Instead she had a surprise.

Ever the artist, the great lady delighted me with "Myself as Cat." Yep. Those are Divine Asta's immense eyes; she is a white cat (a white nubby cloth) with a red heart hanging from a small red collar about her neck. She sits beside an all-black-nubby-fabric male cat whose back is to us. Next to the lovers is a pot of brilliant flowers.

How could I not include this memory in the book?

Advancing in age, the only good thing about it is that rather than traveling through life like a train hurrying along, leaving station after station behind, one can grow like a tree, adding ring upon ring of memory.

It's all there. The day before yesterday is as close and as fresh as the first bloom of youth. ◈

Asta Nielsen "Myself As Cat"

Chapter 11
The Baroness Tossed Me Out

There are two books published in my lifetime I wish I wrote: *Seven Gothic Tales* by Isak Dinesen and *Dandelion Wine* by Ray Bradbury, both bursting with otherworldly lyrical light. The Bradbury, since, like Doug (read: Ray), I too grew up in a small-town community and was a pretty dreamy kid. The Dinesen, since she used language in a way that totally levitates the reader. After I read these writers in college, I felt I was floating. What a way with words!

At Cornell, I had as instructor none other than Vladimir Nabokov, the author of *Lolita*. He taught us that every word must be chosen with precise care, as when Dickens in *Bleak House* chooses to say the grass was green when anybody knows grass is green. Turn back a page, Nabokov told us. It was raining. Thus, after a rain, grass is especially green.

And in the deep springtime gorges of Ithaca, New York, I picked wildflowers with another favorite, Katherine Anne Porter, whose *Pale Horse, Pale Rider* is one fine novella. And when our writing group learned Dylan Thomas was about to be at Syracuse University, we sneaked away on a blustery snow-swirling evening, nearly all of us underage, to meet with the Welsh poet and quaff beer with him at a local pub. Maybe I hoped some of this immense talent might rub off. On me. (Dylan Thomas! Did you ever hear him read aloud? He makes Maya Angelou seem to be an amateur.)

Some celebrities you ought not to meet. They don't, in real life, live up to their own high standards. Once, when I lived in the Big Apple, I saved five dollars to go up to Rumpelmeyer's for an ice-cream soda. It was mid-afternoon; I was sitting by myself. In stepped Joan Blondell with her sister Gloria. I had no doubt who they were. They deposited their graceful selves a few seats away, chatting quietly.

I did not care to intrude, but wished mightily to let Joan Blondell know I was an admirer. I owned a 16mm print of *42nd Street* and remembered a line when Ruby Keeler encounters Dick Powell at a soda fountain. Quickly, I turned to the ladies and spoke Keeler's opening line; Joan Blondell smiled and replied with Powell's line. That was all. What a sweetheart. The exchange was enough.

Joan Blondell liked strawberry ice cream soda and she had a nimble wit. Now, to my sorrow, Isak Dinesen was something else.

I first met her at a ballet function in Copenhagen when I was on my Fulbright at the University. I was wearing a bright red vest with genuine gold buttons. Perhaps it was that which caught her attention.

(An old Jewish man, a survivor from the Holocaust, told me, "Always wear something of value—if the Nazis come, you can run over the border with it." Bad luck. Later, my mother, finding my collection of vests in a closet, threw them away, not knowing the gold buttons were real. For years I had one nice gray wool jacket and by changing vests hoped to give the effect of many outfits.)

Isak Dinesen (Baroness Karen Blixen-Finecke) as "Pierrot"
Photo by Rie Nissen, Copenhagen

Here was the stupendous Isak Dinesen herself. I was young and skinny. Maybe she liked the gold buttons; maybe she thought I was cute. It was a gala party, and she wore a purple wig...fanciful, just like her. I adored *Out of Africa* and *Seven Gothic Tales* with a grand passion. It wasn't hard to imagine her grace, her kindness, and her gentle spirit which shine off the pages of her stories.

Flash forward two years. I was a graduate student at the University of Michigan when I had a cablegram saying: AM DYING. WISH TO DICTATE LAST TALES. PLEASE COME. KAREN BLIXEN. For the Baroness Karen Blixen-Finecke was Isak Dinesen.

It was a command I had to obey. So I sold my Chevy coupe, the only car I ever owned, to buy an air ticket back to beautiful, fairytale Denmark. My family supposed I had lost my marbles. Only Aunt Arlene had heard of her. I can't tell you how eagerly I looked forward to being under the same roof with the enchantress.

I arrived at Kastrup Airport, a bitter cold March morning. I bought an Olivetti portable to tackle the job. I wasn't a professional typist; I don't take shorthand. But surely she'd let me carry pages back each day to Copenhagen to correct them in the event I didn't stay at her house.

A large person in a pink plastic crash helmet strode in my direction and introduced herself as the Countess Dorrit Oxholm. She would take me, she said, on a motorcycle to Rungsted where Isak Dinesen lived.

"I'll take the train," I muttered weakly. I changed dollars to kroner and bought two dozen yellow roses. The train trip was a forty-minute journey. When I got off, a hard March wind whooshed over from Sweden. It was Sunday. Ominous silence, save for the gusts of wind and a strong one stripped the petals off my roses. Stubbornly, I held onto them and arrived at the front door holding a bouquet of empty stems.

I handed them to a maid in a frilly French cap. She sniffed and informed me I was to go around to a back entrance. She reappeared there and steered me inside toward a thick oaken doorway. In days of yore the house had been an inn and had been the residence of Johannes Evald, the finest Danish lyric poet; another great poet, Adam Oelenschlager, had also lived at "Rungstedlund."

The doorway led into a vast room that was formerly a dining hall. The room was dark and as I entered I stumbled over a dog the size of a St. Bernard. His name was Trofast which is Danish for "Fido." He groaned lazily and fell back into a deep snooze much to my relief.

A pitch-black room, curtains closed. So I didn't notice a tiny frail figure in shadow at the far end until a voice barked, "Once upon a time!" and she began telling me a story, a *Last Tale*.

I pulled out my Olivetti, leaped to the nearby table and began typing madly away. No hello, glad to see you, how was your trip, are you hungry. Somebody told me townsfolk called her a witch. After I got adjusted to the gloom, I could see a gaunt figure with orbs like blazing lumps of coal. She wore a silk scarf over her head, tied as a turban.

Since I wasn't invited to stay there, I checked into a cheap pension hotel. Each day I arrived by train, then sat about thirty feet from the lady. No Olivetti. I was told to use her massive and rickety 1929 Remington and was to deliver a letter-perfect pile of pages. As each page was typed, the maid hurried it to the end of the long room. The Baroness took a pencil, gritted her teeth and marked mistakes. There were phrases in Latin, French, German, plus Danish names I never heard of and had to guess the spelling.

If I came to the end of a page, she cried, "You can't stop there!" So I began to use not the usual typing paper but legal-size; that gave another minute or two before the awful moment of pulling out the page and inserting a new sheet.

I was too scared or too much in awe to ask for such a mundane item as money. Therefore, I sold my return ticket. At the pension hotel breakfast was included: bread, cheese, runny soft-boiled egg and strong coffee. Often, that was the day's diet. Eventually, I lost thirty pounds and literally was fading away.

I would arrive at Rungstedlund, type up her words in a frenzy and depart without a complaint. The old woman is ill and dying, I was reminded. Humor her. Don't forsake her. I was a servant without pay.

Like her brother Thomas, I was to enter at the trade entrance. According to her faithful companion, Clara Svendsen, the last male visitors welcome at the front door were Truman Capote and Tennessee Williams.

One morning came a phone call, an inquiry from the States: there could be a film of *Out of Africa* with Garbo portraying her. To me, this was exciting. "Who is this Gree-ta Garbo?" she sneered.

As a youngster I read that when Selznick filmed part of *Portrait of Jenny* in Central Park, Garbo was at a party gazing out the window, observing the commotion below. "It looks silly," she

The Baroness Tossed Me Out   171

told Leonard Lyons. Someone put on a Bing Crosby record. "Who is this Bing Crosby?" she wondered. I should have asked Bing if he heard of Isak Dinesen. There was only one film star worth anything, the Baroness stated. That was Emil Jannings.

Another call. From the Swedish director Alf Sjöberg, inquiring about availability of her tale *Sorrow-Acre*. Zero interest. Movies, humbug.

There is one nice memory.

She wanted to wear a costume she wore to a court ball long ago, of Pierrot. Or was it Columbine? An inch of makeup got applied to her thin dry skin—parchment stretched on brittle bones. A car was rented. Off we went to the Royal Court photographer in Copenhagen.

For a full hour she was young once again, chatting, being charming. How I wished that day had lasted longer. Clara Svendsen must have also.

Dinesen asked if I knew any American Negro jazz musicians. I didn't. Would some boys from the ballet do, said I, feeling like a pimp. She definitely had a sensual side for I saw some marvelous oil paintings she had done when she had her coffee farm in Kenya—of her lithe and lean houseboys whom, Clara Svendsen revealed, went about the place naked.

On a fatal morning I misspelled two words. You must understand these were gothic tales, these *Last Tales*. I never had a chance to sit back to enjoy nuances of style or overall beauty of narrative. I was too busy typing sheer sounds and making sure to spell "color" in the British way, "colour."

Once, she asked for the English name for a many-layered cloak young men of fashion wore to the opera in 1800. She made a little pencil drawing on a napkin. It looked like a Christmas tree. I wracked my brain, coming up with a weak entry: a havelock (from Dickens)—in actuality a traveling cape. "*That* you should *know!*" she screeched. We had to carry her up to bed.

Under the circumstances, on the whole, I did a pretty fair job. She would talk until growing tired, beckoning me to vanish. No opportunity to correct anything. The agony of *Last Tales* was almost over. Although they proved not to be the last inasmuch as she later journeyed to Italy, was revived in the warm sunshine and wrote more books.

Now please recall that in Rungsted she was not known as Karen Blixen-Finecke, her real name. No, she was *heksen*, the witch.

One special morning she announced she craved some nourishment and the maid brought mashed potatoes and tea. For me, a rare treat—a piece of bread, tea in a small cup. *Harper's Bazaar* said she dined exclusively on grapes or oysters or chestnuts and drank nothing but champagne.

The next instant is etched forever in my stomach, for she decided to continue the dictation. "*Witch!*" she said. Dutifully I typed; after all, it was a gothic tale. And she went on, "Which is to say…"

Oh oh. Gulping, I scratched out "Witch" and penciled in the proper word, "Which." But she caught it and marked it and threw down the sheet of paper delivered by the maid from my table to her at the end of the room. That was it. "You have no feeling whatsoever for literature!"

Next morning, I was eating my soft-boiled egg when there was a knock at my door. Clara Svendsen, her companion, was on

Jan Wahl, a dozen years later, still spooked by his literary adventure
Photo by Mogens Gad, Copenhagen

the hall phone. Clara heaved a sigh. "You did your best." Then she added that the Baroness had found a sailor to replace me.

Weeks after this, Clara telephoned again. The great lady was invited to Russia by the poet Boris Pasternak. Will I please come along to carry her on and off the trains and troikas? The chance to meet Pasternak, the writer of *Doctor Zhivago*, was tempting. "I'm not that crazy," I replied.

Yet Isak Dinesen may have had warmer feelings for me than I knew. A package arrived in Copenhagen with an inscribed *Out of Africa* and one of the photographs by Rie Nissen. Both of them I guard with my life. Before I left, I confided to her that I also hoped to be a published writer.

"Don't write!" she grumbled. I suppose she meant the life of a writer is never easy. I like to think that's what she meant. But she might at least have offered me lunch.

Chapter 12
Movie Stars to Meet In Heaven:
Rudolph Valentino, Mary Pickford, Douglas Fairbanks, Colleen Moore

Rudolph Valentino (1895-1926)

Why do I want to meet him?

Because he dared to be the first male heartthrob, despite some smarty-pants calling him a pink powderpuff.

Valentino! Now there's a legendary name if ever was one. He was a perplexing new kind of personality. Brutal, tender, insecure, arrogant, sensual. His lovemaking suggested there was pleasure to it. Maybe this was too much for macho men of the Twenties to endure, but the ladies adored him.

The male audience may have reviled him, yet they copied him. Sideburns were suddenly "in" and so was oiled or brilliantined hair. Wristwatches had been only for sissies. When Valentino sported one, they flew off the shelves.

His willingness to show passion and vulnerability may have disturbed the ordinary guy, nevertheless he was imitated.

And he revolutionized the movie business and thereby American culture.

When at age 17 Valentino left Italy, he went to Paris, then to America in hopes of finding his fortune. Hard luck in New York

Rudolph Valentino, circa 1922

made him temporarily a part-time landscape gardener, a tea dancer, an escort for prosperous widows.

He recalled: "My hotel room at 43rd and Broadway was a skylight cubbyhole for storing brooms. I washed in a mop sink, dried on newspaper, and could not raise two dollars weekly rental. Next came a 12 cent a night room, and then a Central Park bench."

His ability as a dancer saved him. Eventually, he danced his way to the West Coast and ultimately he caught the eye of influential June Mathis at Metro, who picked him for the epic *Four Horsemen of the Apocalypse*. His tango dazzled the ladies; that tango took the world by storm. So did Rudy.

In honor of this new star a Dane, Jacob Gade, composed a tango in 1922, "Jealousy." The family made so much money from "Jealousy," they were able to buy a castle built by Tycho Brae.

Soon came *The Sheik*, or "Sheek," if you prefer. And *Blood and Sand* and *Monsieur Beaucaire*. Too bad Ernst Lubitsch didn't helm *Beaucaire*. For this opulent production Rudy got Sydney Olcott, who somehow missed the intent of Booth Tarkington's novel.

Rudy's wife Natacha Rambova spent a fortune on lace and gorgeous silks or satins, on bejeweled garters and buckles, on chandeliers, on polished marble. Most audiences overlooked how witty and seductive he was, how he mocked himself.

In this and in *The Eagle* (after a tale by Pushkin) and most of all, in *Son of the Sheik* he was truly light on his feet and heavy with the charm. His only rival was Ramon Navarro, who also moved with a dancer's grace. Rudy's eroticism, however, was unique.

Perhaps when he died tragically and prematurely of peritonitis, after completing *Son of the Sheik*, it was a relief to movie-going males.

In the Thirties, he was replaced by the tough guy: by Cagney, Clark Gable, Spencer Tracy. Only Tyrone Power (who did a new *Blood and Sand* in Technicolor) somehow shares some of his qualities. Really, Rudolph Valentino stands alone.

As Valentino lay dying in agony in a New York City hospital, he asked the doctor, "Did I behave like a pink powder puff?"

Valentino in *The Four Horsemen of the Apocalypse* (1921)

Mary Pickford (1893-1979)

Why do I want to meet her?

Because she didn't want to grow up and, since she was tremendously successful at it, she made millions; and happened to become the world's sweetheart.

She could play comedy—her preference. Equally effectively, she could do heavy drama. She was the most famous woman on this planet. Charlie Chaplin was the most famous man. Like him, she seems more at home in vehicles where she resides on the other side of the tracks.

With Pickford, it was more than those shining golden curls.

She was best known playing not quite a child, not quite yet a woman. She lived in a never-neverland beyond sex and age, suspended in time by sheer will and chutzpah.

Like D. W. Griffith's impression of Lillian Gish, she was truly non-sexual and virginal—never considered a threat to flesh-and-blood women. She was adorable Little Mary.

At the beginning, she worked with Griffith and made one-reelers at Biograph. At least one of them was a kind of fairytale, *Lena and the Geese* in 1912, although her most famous Biograph was her last, *The New York Hat*, written by another girl, Anita Loos, who was paid ten dollars.

She moved upward. In 1914 she convinced an otherwise canny Adolph Zukor to pay her 50% of her films' profits. In that year she made two inept features by pioneer Edwin S. Porter, *Cinderella* and *Tess of the Storm Country*. In the latter she portrayed a tomboy.

By 1917 she was finding herself as *Rebecca of Sunnybrook Farm* and *Poor Little Rich Girl*; at last she had skilled directors (Marshall

Mary Pickford, circa 1918

Neilan and Maurice Tourneur). The latter helped bring out her innermost self. Best of all, made certain she got lit and photographed to perfection.

In *The Little Princess* (also 1917) and *Amarilly of Clothes-Line Alley* (1918) and *Daddy Long Legs* (1919), Mary captured the hearts of a love-struck public.

In two features she spread her wings, acting two parts simultaneously thanks to the camera magic of expert Charles Rosher. In *Stella Maris* (1918) she was both a cockney orphan, homely-as-sin Unity Blake, and the spoiled invalid, pretty Stella Maris; one dies, one lives. In *Little Lord Fauntleroy* (1921) she was both pampered Cedric *and* his mother, Dearest, who tells him—"Cedric, I cannot bear to have you grow up."

And Mary didn't. As late as the spirited *Little Annie Rooney* of 1925 or the beautifully photographed *Sparrows* of 1926 in which she was an ageless child with maternal instincts.

I watched Jean Arthur fly as Peter Pan at age forty-five (Boris Karloff was Captain Hook—what a bonanza). However, that was theater. In movies the camera can be merciless, hard to convince. Defying it was the triumph of Little Mary.

Her brother Jack, a charismatic lad, was able to do something Mary couldn't: he played Pip in *Great Expectations*; he was *Freckles* and *Tom Sawyer*. 1917 was a hallmark year for the Pickfords.

No child at negotiating, in 1919 Mary, with future husband Doug Fairbanks and Griffith and Chaplin, formed United Artists. Her first release with the company was *Pollyanna*.

If she had quit after cutting off the curls in the delightful *My Best Girl* in 1927, she would have ended on a high note. After sound came in, she chose to remake two Norma Talmadge successes. *Kiki* had proved Norma a brilliant comedienne, frolicking with Ronald Colman. Mary's foil was Reginald Denny. Better than *Kiki* was Mary's *Secrets*; she took on Leslie Howard.

Then she had a glorious stroke of genius: she resolved to do *Alice in Wonderland* in three-strip Technicolor—with Disney. Negotiations dragged on.

Meanwhile, Paramount jumped in with a dreadful attempt to conquer Lewis Carroll, despite Gary Cooper as The White Knight, W.C. Fields as Humpty Dumpty.

Pickford in *Suds* (1920)

Too bad. Preparatory photos reveal, at age forty-one, she looked terrific. Again she didn't have to grow up.

We were denied what might have been the jewel in her crown.

Douglas Fairbanks (1883-1939)

Why do I want to meet him?

Because he brought a new kind of fun—he was the first Zorro, D'Artagnan, first Robin Hood and Thief of Bagdad; he was a pirate, too.

Doug was the answer to every kid's dream. He made storybooks come alive by inventing the swashbuckler movie. He was an adventurer, the knight smarter than any villain, his feats of derring-do a joy to see.

Jane Austen described three sisters. One moved slowly, one was a bustler. The third moved in a slow bustle. Most of us get from "A" to "B" by walking or running. Doug did it by springing, bouncing, bustling, leaping. He was lighter than air.

No other movie actor ever equaled his athletic charm—his easy physical grace. A Fairbanks set was one of silly jokes, hijinks, boisterous behavior. He loved to arrive at the studio in totally inappropriate costume. His restless personality was tamed by channeling energy into his screen character.

In his early features, he was an optimistic Yankee, a madcap Manhattanite. Fairbanks liked to contrast the narrow deep canyons of Wall Street with the openness of Arizona and its unspoiled landscape.

Douglas Fairbanks, circa 1916

D.W. Griffith, director, and Fairbanks, the actor, made movies respectable. In February of 1915 regular theater prices were charged for *The Birth of the Nation* while in September of the same year Fairbanks' first Triangle feature, *The Lamb*, was offered at $3 a ticket.

Doug's films during WWI and beyond were taken as a tonic. He made audiences feel good. They adored the Fairbanks grin. And he wrote inspirational books giving advice such as "To blazes with worrying about WHY things happen. Just make the best of everything, face life with a smile, and above all, don't take anything too seriously."

It was he who unearthed in a pulp magazine, *All-Story Weekly*, "The Curse of Capistrano." He gave it a better title, *The Mark of Zorro*. This tale of early 1800s California fitted Doug Fairbanks like a glove. He found an outlet for all that energy.

Besides producing, he provided the scenarios for *The Mollycoddle* (1920), *Robin Hood* (1922), *The Black Pirate* (1926), *The Gaucho* (1927), and *The Iron Mask* (1929).

His splendid physique is on display in the spectacle *The Thief of Bagdad* (1924) with mind-boggling sets that William Cameron Menzies provided. Lithe and lean, oozing health, Doug had plenty of space to leap into.

To film-goers' delight, Mary Pickford had become his wife. Her stepson, Doug, Jr., referred to her as a "miniaturist." Doug, of course, thought big.

Mary was the money-minded one, yet Doug was shrewd in business. And together, Doug and Mary were Hollywood's royalty. An invitation to Pickfair was an honor. At one of their dinners you might see Albert Einstein, Jack Dempsey or Winston

Fairbanks in *The Thief of Bagdad* (1924)

Churchill. Parlor games, mind games, practical jokes, no liquor. Doug and Mary did not go out. People came to them.

Doug and Mary were the perfect couple; that's what America wanted to believe. But it was an illusion just like the movies.

Chaplin, Doug's friend (not Mary's), compared their marriage to Peter Pan and Wendy. Doug, Jr., a sharp observer of character, referred to his father as "a series of masks."

At heart, though, I think Douglas Fairbanks was mostly a small boy, dressed in splendid costumes of yore, simply having lots and lots of fun.

Don't you?

Colleen Moore (1900-1988)

Why do I want to meet her?

Because her look and spirit represent what we love about the Twenties, resulting in F. Scott Fitzgerald naming her the ultimate flapper.

To be more precise, what the author of *The Great Gatsby* said was, "I was the spark that lit up Flaming Youth. Colleen Moore was the torch." And there you have it from the horse's mouth. F. Scott Fitzgerald practically invented the Twenties.

Colleen Moore was The Flapper, Valentino was The Sheik. How to explain the term "flapper"? Seems a lady went about in all sorts of weather in rubber galoshes, leaving the metal buckles unbuckled, resulting in a delightful flapping sound.

Now, thinking flapper, Louise Brooks may have been more gorgeous; Joan Crawford, she of *Our Dancing Daughters* (1928) and *Our Modern Maidens* (1929), shook the meanest Charleston; and lovely Laura La Plante, sporting a chic blonde bob, was more sophisticated. Clara Bow? Clara Bow was no flapper. Clara Bow was Clara Bow.

No, the girl who put twinkle in *Twinkletoes* was Colleen Moore—more nice than naughty, more sweet than sassy. Colleen or Laura you could take home to Mom. You might not trust Dad with Joan or Clara. Sue Carol fits in there somewhere.

Colleen Moore, circa 1922

You've got to have affection for anyone who makes an early start with a film titled *Egg Crate Wallop* (1919). I have no notion what that means. You tell me. Her introduction to Hollywood is well known—D.W. Griffith owed her uncle a favor. The master's instinct was off-kilter that day. He didn't use Colleen, instead handed her on. Worse, when Dorothy Gish presented Rudolph Valentino to him, Griffith dismissed him. "Too foreign."

Listen to this litany of Colleen Moore oeuvres, after she paid her dues as ingénue to Tom Mix and Charles Ray. *Flaming Youth*

Moore in *Her Wild Oat* (1928)

Moore's dollhouse library's porch

(1923), *Painted People, The Perfect Flapper, Flirting with Love* (all 1924), *Sally, We Moderns* (1925), *It Must Be Love* (1926), *Orchids and Ermine, Naughty But Nice* (1927), *Her Wild Oat, Happiness Ahead* (1928), *Synthetic Sin, Why Be Good?* (1929). The titles tell all.

However, Colleen tried other roles during that period—*So Big* (after the Edna Ferber novel), *Ella Cinders* (after the comic strip), *Lilac Time* (where she was a French lass in WWI pursued by an American, Gary Cooper). In *Twinkletoes* (1926) she played a street urchin in London's Limehouse; she had some of the innocence of Miss Gish as in *Broken Blossoms*, but more of the spunkiness of Mary Pickford in *Suds*.

She had her own production company; it was headed by her husband. She was First National's prime moneymaker. In 1926 and 1927 Colleen Moore was voted by theater owners the number one attraction.

Offscreen, Colleen was a mixture of irresistible Twinkletoes and carefree flapper. In *Silent Star*, her autobiography, she tells of a shindig held at Sam Goldwyn's house. Suddenly, at the door appeared F. Scott Fitzgerald with his Zelda. They were on all fours, barking loudly: "Please, can we come to your party? We're strangers and don't know anyone!"

True, the lady may not have been a pinup like Betty Grable of the fabulous gams, but those Irish eyes (one blue, one brown) showed sparkle and spunk. The Twenties was not about legs. Legs were for dancing. The Twenties was about stamina and a ride in a roadster and oh-you-kid.

Hollywood was inventive in those days. Tom Mix tooled about in a robin's egg-blue Rolls-Royce. Pola Negri walked a leopard on a leash. Beloved Roscie Arbuckle invited everybody to the

Fairmont. When the Twenties were done and gone, the flapper died, too—stale as yesterday's bathtub gin. Jolly while it lasted.

Besides defining the character of the flapper, Colleen Moore left a permanent legacy. You can find her incredible dollhouse today at the Museum of Science and Industry in Chicago.

Since childhood she had a taste for miniatures of all kinds, so she decided to build a castle on a scale of one inch to the foot. It took seven years to complete, from 1928 to 1935, and cost a half-million dollars. Artisans throughout the world contributed to it. It holds over two thousand objects, most of them unique.

The chandeliers are real diamonds; it has running water, is constructed of aluminum and can be taken apart for shipping; even so, it weighs over a ton. It was designed by set designer Harold Grieve, husband of Jetta Goudal. A dollhouse without dolls—the idea being the observer must imagine its inhabitants.

The tiny autograph album in the library was signed by Herbert Hoover, F.D.R., Richard Nixon, Winston Churchill, Charles de Gaulle, Nehru, Douglas MacArthur, Frank Lloyd Wright, John Glenn, Paderewski, Henry Ford, J.P. Morgan, Pablo Picasso, Madam Chiang Kai-shek. The owner always regretted that she failed to get J.F.K.

Nevertheless, that all these important people wanted to be included is proof of the esteem in which Colleen Moore and her famous castle are held.

A million viewers a year pay tribute to the torch that lit up Flaming Youth.

Chapter 13
Postcards from Leni

Pavlov's dog trick: say Leni Riefenstahl. Bingo! Holocaust and Hitler. Worse, with a tagline: "Hitler's Filmmaker."
Is this fair, I wonder?

A friend of mine happened to be born in 1930's Berlin. Her parents fled from the Nazi wrath. This friend said her Toledo rabbi told the congregation that L.R. made in 1940 a one-hour documentary comparing Jews to rats and the bubonic plague. I'd seen this abomination. I replied that the rabbi was misinformed. A contemporary of Riefenstahl's, a man, concocted that awful garbage.

"You're calling the rabbi a liar?" my friend cried.

"Misinformed," I repeated.

So I wrote a piece I hope was open-minded, and mailed it off with two of my books in German editions to Frau Riefenstahl who was living at Poecking, near Munich and engaged on a substantial project, an underwater color feature she never completed—although she lived to be one hundred. Even Leni Riefenstahl couldn't live forever, yet she gave it a good try.

She responded at once, thanking me by eventually sending postcards from sea-locations around the globe: from the Maldives, from Indonesia, from Papua, New Guinea.

194   Through a Lens Darkly

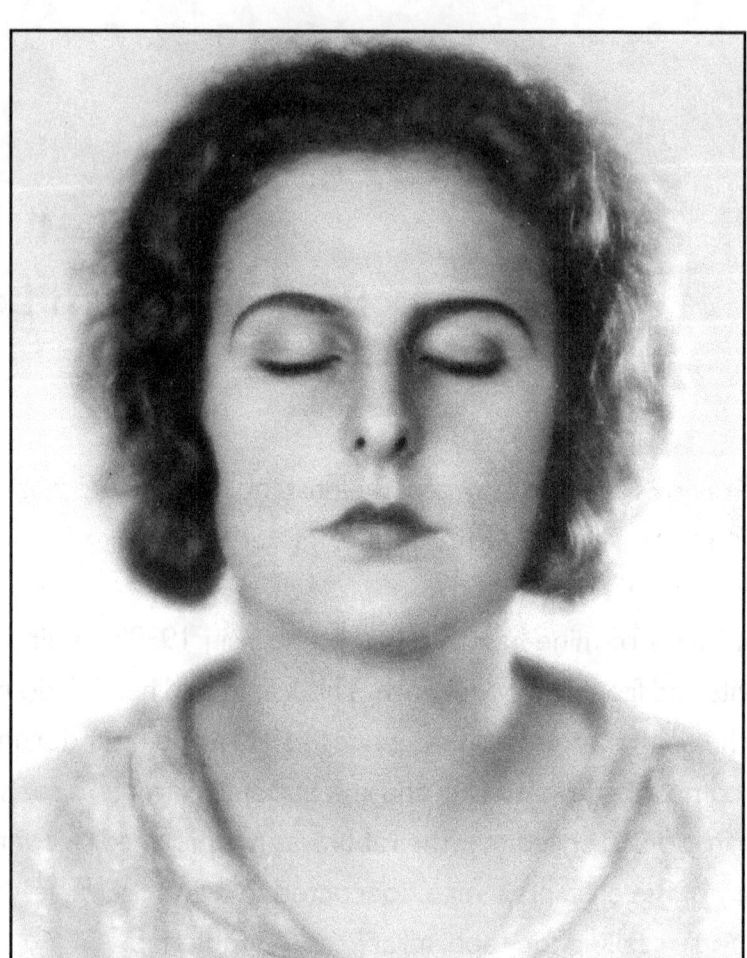

Leni Riefenstahl in *The White Hell of Pitz Palu* (1929)

The first message was from Costa Rica. "Since several weeks I live on a diving boat and I dive around the famous island 'cocos.' This island is the dream of all good divers...because here exist still a lot of Hammerheads and other big fishes. The diving here is unique. Not easy, because the water is very cool, the currents strong and often high waves. But for camera good."

What she left out was that underwater she felt better, since she suffered from severe arthritis. Generously, she sent along photos and video cassettes of her fiction films *The Blue Light* and *Tiefland*.

I kept my pen pal a secret from acquaintances in Germany, all of them in some way connected to films. Her name was anathema.

A few years back in Hamburg, I learned there was an exhibition of her underwater photos at a walk-up art gallery in a remote corner of the city. You'd suppose I wanted a rendezvous with the Devil.

I managed to find the show with its large stunning compositions radiating dazzling colors of corals, rare fishes and urchins, amazing views from the deepest arena of the sea, brought to light by one the most renowned of 20th-century photographers.

There's Steichen and Stieglitz at the start, Riefenstahl at the close—all triumphant artists.

For she was prodigiously talented, early on a highly regarded modern dancer, then as an athlete, a skier, a mountain climber, becoming an actress evolving into a skilled director of epic proportions.

Leni Riefenstahl is the most remarkable film cutter in cinema history. Following the war, she seemed smashed by Fate itself—a reputation in tatters, her health impaired, her body broken after several accidents. Yet again and again, she rose like a Phoenix bird from the ashes.

After starring in a number of mountain films by Dr. Arnold Fanck, she directed her first feature, the mystical *The Blue Light* in 1932. She played Junta, an innocent girl fascinated by a strange glow coming from crystals of a nearby mountain. To superstitious villagers, Junta is a witch, an outsider. She meets a tragic end.

Hitler insisted L.R. was the one for the job, to make a film of the mammoth rally to be held at Nuremberg. She countered by insisting she had other priorities, other plans. However, the challenge appealed to her and she agreed.

Remember—Germany was humbled by its defeat in the Great War and by the Treaty of Versailles as set down by the Allies. Guess who flies to the rescue? *The Triumph of the Will*, as the film was called, opens with Hitler in a plane up in the clouds over the city. A hundred thousand of the faithful await him, goosesteppers and Party members, anxious for the Fuehrer.

Music by Herbert Windt lets you know something *big* is afoot.

Hitler's trick is to surround himself with followers mediocre as himself—those willing to bow to empty rhetoric. Riefenstahl's cameras catch it: lets us gasp at the madness of Hitler shouting and haranguing and barking. Handsome youths march in perfect step. Tens of thousands cheer themselves hoarse. The effect is hair-raising—scarier than *Nosferatu* or *Caligari*. And as Hannah Arendt was to put it later, shows the banality of evil.

I watched *Triumph* in a pristine complete original. Once was plenty. I had to get rid of it. Unbearable proof what a nutcake the guy was. How did millions fall under his spell? If Frau R. herself got hypnotized, she paid a price many times over. We ought to thank her, for *Triumph* is an extraordinary experience.

A more stupendous project lay ahead.

Although expecting to embark upon *Penthesilea*, after a famous play by Kleist, to render in visual terms his beautiful words, a story about the Queen of the Amazons and the hero Achilles, she was asked instead to document the Berlin Olympic Games of 1936.

Riefenstahl: *Olympia* Part One, "The Festival of the People" (1938)

Penthesilea must wait. Yes, she'd make *Olympia*. In total, 1,300,000 feet of film were shot, truly dwarfing Eisenstein and his *Que Viva Mexico!* footage. She spent two years assembling and editing.

She made two films from it, Part One, "The Festival of the People," and Part Two, "The Festival of Beauty."

The prolog to each shows naked athletes exercising or at play—noble statues come to life. The Marathon Race that closes

Part One and the Diving Sequence near the end of Part Two are film-editing magic.

Techniques she invented for *Triumph* and *Olympia* have never been surpassed. The camera crew for *Olympia* consisted of about fifty men, including *Caligari's* Willy Hameister. They filmed 136 competitions. Riefenstahl decided what lenses or filters were used, what kind of film stock, the camera speed, where every camera was placed or how it was to be moved. You don't have to be sports-minded to thrill to all this.

Leni Riefenstahl had two masters, G.W. Pabst and Dr. Fanck (who co-directed *The White Hell of Pitz Palu* in 1929—she appeared with Gustav Diessl) and surpassed them both.

Art critic Clive Bell maintained that a work of art ought to be judged on its merits, not by its historical context; art for art's sake. L.R. always claimed she was apolitical.

At the height of Nazi madness, she dared to commence the black-and-white *Tiefland* ("Lowlands") whose subject was not to Goebbels' liking: gypsies. She was to play the lead, a gypsy dancer. (The aborted *Penthesilea* she hoped to make in color.) *Tiefland*, like *Blue Light*, had at its theme the beauty of nature opposed to the imperfections of mankind. She was not able to finish this film until ten years later.

American and French authorities, at war's end, held her for years and her negatives were confiscated—among them, material from which she needed to edit *Tiefland*. Fifty times (!) she went to court. Fifty times it was proven that she was not a member of the Party, nor was there suspicion of guilt. A claim she had a special relationship to Hitler was unfounded.

Regarding the charge that both the Nuremberg Rally and Olympic Games films were commissioned to create propaganda, the courts said her efforts were "aimed at producing a documentary." *Triumph* in 1935 received a gold medal from France and Grand Prize at the Venice Film Festival.

Olympia won Grand Prize at Venice in 1938, and in 1939 got the Diploma for the Olympic Gold Medal. The legal ruling for it stated it was "an international concern and therefore eliminated itself as an incriminating work." These two commissions "do not by themselves constitute making propaganda for the National Socialists."

The courts concluded that she accepted these commissions "only under pressure, and therefore in no way wrangled improper benefits for herself."

Nonetheless, rumors and attacks grew relentlessly. Italian communists called her "one of Hitler's favorites," while to *Paris Soir* she was the "Pompadour of the Third Reich." The result was that investors pulled out of a pet project on which she'd spent two years in preparation.

So she switched gears and at age sixty went to live among the Nuba tribe in Sudan, and learned their language. From this, she produced two exquisite volumes of color photos, again celebrating the magnificence of the human body.

Forty years later, she was still active—then on her underwater filming, a labor of some thirty years. This, despite crippling infirmities, including broken bones from a helicopter crash (at age ninety-seven) when she was returning to the beloved Nuba.

In 1995, the Goethe Institute in San Francisco invited her as a special guest and I was asked to bring prints of two features, *The White Hell of Pitz Palu* and *S.O.S. Iceberg!* and there was to be a gala dinner. However, threatening calls were made to the Institute; she was advised to withdraw.

Riefenstahl in *S.O.S. Iceberg* (1933)

She had come to the States in 1938 and was here during the infamous Crystal Night. She could not get a public showing of *Olympia* and only Walt Disney among Hollywood moguls agreed to meet with her. In the mid-1960s she returned, once more seeking a distributor for *Olympia*. At the Library of Congress, to her dismay, she learned that Raymond Rohauer had gotten there first and had taken a copyright *in his name* on her film. I am told her screams were heard up and down the hallowed halls.

Despite these fiascos, including the disappointment at the Goethe Institute, in 1997 Cinecon, the L.A. convention for movie buffs, bit the bullet. She was invited and, indeed, she appeared. The visit was a resounding success, despite a few raised voices, and she graciously signed photos, stills, and her autobiography for hours in a firm, clear hand.

With *Schindler's List* (and many programs on the History Channel), issues related to the Third Reich again are hot. L.R. is "Hitler's Filmmaker." Aside from the lady returning to Germany in 1938, attempting to continue working (*Tiefland*), what many find her guilty of is turning a blind eye to the evils of Nazism. What she knew or didn't know we'll never know.

I was a child during WWII. A couple from our neighborhood suddenly was gone. Kim and her husband were Americans—yet after Pearl Harbor, were no longer considered as such. They were removed to a mysterious internment camp. Nobody objected.

They, and thousands of "Nisei," had funny and suspicious eyes. So livelihood was denied them, property confiscated, dignity taken away. An old "Nisei" I met told me that at his camp he was given only one sheet of toilet paper per day. Unbelievable. The old man hung his head remembering the past.

Leni Riefenstahl: "My work today" (1995)

I can't compare the extent of what Hitler did to Jews, gays, political mavericks or others to how we treated those of Japanese ancestry—but you get my drift?

Seems our government, with silent consent from taxpayers, did not think the "Nisei" solution wrong. I doubt German officials in public or at home were discussing the removal of the Jews.

Triumph of the Will is a spellbinding documentary. Witness to insanity.

Olympia goes out of the way to extol brotherhood and sisterhood or our human race—beyond boundary, race or creed. Its Diving Sequence is one of the finest moments in cinema—shots cut together of divers, men and women from all nations (doesn't matter from what country), flowing, flying into a seamless whole.

Tiefland is a romantic tragedy celebrating gypsy spirit in Spain at the time of Goya.

These are her poisonous productions?

You tell me, if you or your family is old enough: did you or they know about the fire-bombing of Dresden or Hamburg or Tokyo, when a hundred thousand people died on each of these nights? Did you go about as if nothing had happened? What was Riefenstahl's guilt? That Hitler liked her work?

Time ran out at last for Leni Riefenstahl. Maybe now we must say enough already. Stop punishing her for sins of the Third Reich.

At any rate, I cherish photos or postcards she sent. My favorite photo, dated 17 Jan. 95, is inscribed: "My work today." She sits at the editing table, eyes shining, hair bright red—surrounded by four fabulous frames from the never-completed *Underwater Wonders*.

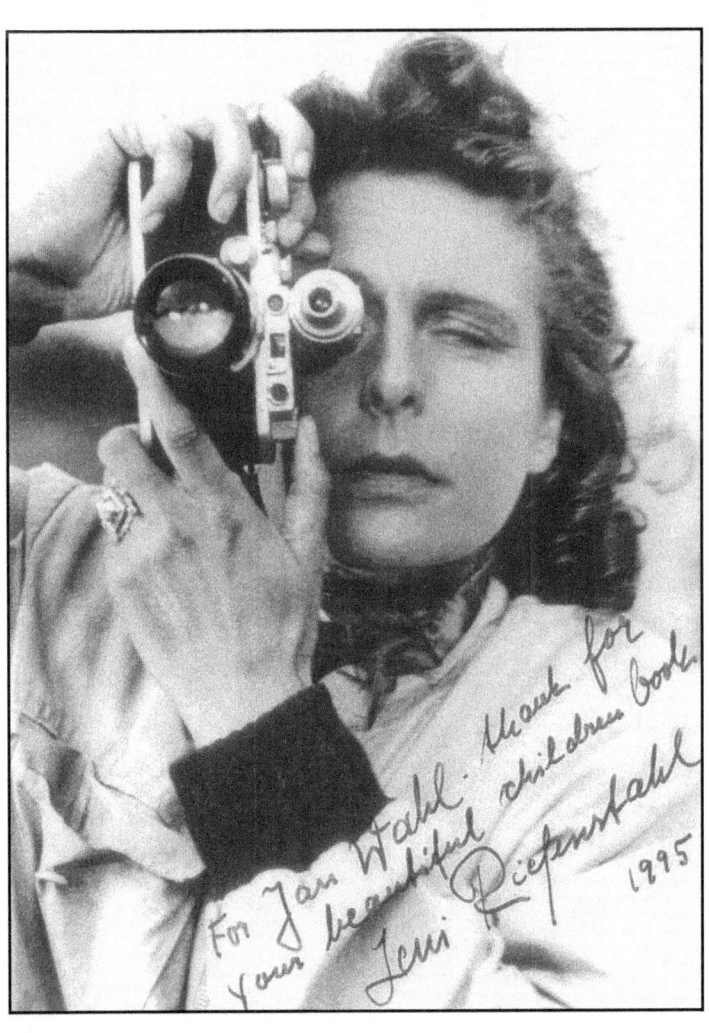

Chapter 14
Looney Tunes and *Happy Harmonies:*
Hugh Harman and Rudolf Ising

A sk an animated-cartoon buff what turns him on. Invariably, as if to say, "Who else?" he names Tex Avery. Hopefully, Chuck Jones.

I'm expecting more.

Maybe Max Fleischer's playful surrealism. Or the best of Disney when artists included Gustav Tenggren, Kay Nielsen, Ferdinand Horvath, Walt Kelly, the Provensens, Hardie Gramatky.

How nice it would be if the buff admitted a fondness for the French-Canadian *Triplets of Belleville* and the Japanese *Tombstone for the Fireflies, My Neighbor Totoro* or *Howl's Moving Castle*. Fresh and inventive. Tex Avery?

If we're speaking of art at all, it's rather like nominating Andy Warhol over Klee or Kandinsky.

Give that buff a super gag and he's in sheer heaven.

If I see the logo of Papa Laemmle's airplane chug-chugging around the globe introducing a Universal Picture, if it's a horror film, I know it has quality. My heart is going pitty pat-pat.

And when I read "Harman-Ising" my expectations are similarly high. For what a team they were!

Interestingly, Ubbe Iwerks (who first drew Mickey Mouse) and Walt Disney (for whom he drew Mickey) were both born in 1901. And Hugh Harman and Rudy Ising were both born in 1903. All four were working in the early Twenties in Kansas City when Disney formed his Laugh-O-Grams Studio. Within a year, there was a reel called *Alice's Wonderland*—a live girl wandering through cartoonland. A live Max Fleischer already was appearing in the *Out of the Inkwell* series.

(For the record, I met a number of Fleischer animators when I lived in Mexico, including my neighbors Earl Klein and his wife Maria. All of them declared Max to be the inspiring force, not brother Dave who tried to take credit after Max's death.)

No question that it is Walt Disney who was the guiding light for his friends Iwerks and Harman and Ising. Not a terrific artist himself but a genius who motivated and kept a tight ship. Remember, these were mere kids: Harman and Ising were just out of their teens.

The *Alice* cartoons are clumsy and primitive, not in the same league with Fleischer's *Out of the Inkwells* or the *Felix the Cat* series from Pat Sullivan's studio—these youngsters were learning by doing.

There was a primer, a how-to-do animated movie book published in 1920; however, Mozart and Mendelssohn probably did not require a textbook in harmony or orchestration. These kids were on their own.

By the fall of 1923, Walt and Company, together with the sample *Alice* reel in tow, moved to California. The rent was $10 a month. A distributor was found, Margaret Winkler, who also distributed Felix. The *Alice* cartoons made up in energy what they might lack in artistry; however, much superior was the next series: *Oswald the Lucky Rabbit*. With long, floppy black ears, carefree manner and mischievous eyes, Oswald reminds me more of Hugh Harman's Bosko than he does Ubbe Iwerks' Mickey in *Plane Crazy*.

Eventually, Ubbe, Hugh and Rudy struck out on their own; Harman and Ising left first. *Oswald* was distributed by Universal through Charles Mintz, husband of Miss Winkler. *Oswald* did not "belong" to Walt Disney, who made sure to hold onto Mickey.

For Pat Powers, Ubbe invented the rather lame Flip the Frog and Willie Whopper, a fat boy who told lies. Neither was earthshaking, although Flip the Frog in *Spooks* (1932) and Willie the Whopper in *Stratos Fear* (1933) and *Cave Man* (1933) are

Rudy Isling's stock certificate for Laugh-O-Gram Films, 1922
(Russell Merritt collection)

topnotch. And he made beautiful use of the limited Cinecolor process in the fairytale cartoons. Iwerks was to do his best efforts at Columbia, under Charles Mintz of all people.

To me, *House on the Merry-Go-Round* is one of the most exciting cartoons—nonstop eye-catching action in saturated Technicolor beyond belief. A boy falls asleep on the merry-go-round and his painted horse gallops, slides and spins through every inch of the fair with cops and crooks in hot pursuit. Ubbe's masterpiece.

In 1928 and 1929, Harman and Ising at the Mintz establishment improved Oswald one hundred percent. Three of their *Oswalds* exist for our pleasure. Of the two I know, *Homeless Homer* is credited to Rudolf Ising while *Sick Cylinders* is credited to Hugh Harman. Both are extraordinary, equal to the bursts of imagination in the best of *Felix the Cat* cartoons from 1928 such as the superlative *Sure-Locked Homes*.

(Another aside. Otto Messmer is today thought of as Felix's true papa. Messmer outlived, by many decades, Pat Sullivan, who died in 1933, with no one to dispute his claim. What bugs me is this. If Messmer was the genius there, why didn't he continue to do work of the same caliber? True, he kept drawing the Felix comic strip wonderfully.

When he did find a new outlet for Felix in 1935 with RKO-Van Beuren, with Technicolor to boot, why were those such poor pallid things, lacking any of the former verve and technique? They weren't as clever as Molly Moo Cow.

In fact, Pat Sullivan himself was an able cartoonist; his early comic strips are excellent. Perhaps in some manner Pat Sullivan was to Felix what Disney was to Mickey?

Lois Hardwick as Alice with Walt Disney in Hollywood (1927)
In back row: Walker Harman, Ubbe Iwerks, Hugh Harman, Rudy Ising, Friz Freleng, and Roy Disney (Russell Merrit collection)

Film history, and animation history most of all, cannot be proved easily. According to historian Bill Blackbeard, around the turn of the last century, years before *Plane Crazy*, there was a Mickey Mouse and his Minnie in an early comic strip. Make of that what you will.

Gertie the Dinosaur, it is often claimed, is the first real American cartoon. It is by Winsor McCay, but even earlier is his *Little Nemo*. And is *The Great Train Robbery* by Edwin S. Porter the first American story film? Hardly. More properly it's Porter's *Jack and the Beanstalk*.)

Well, let's look at these two Harman and Ising *Oswald the Lucky Rabbits*. In the Disney *Oswald* and *Alice* cartoons, not much personality was revealed. Alice was almost a zero. What Harman-Ising seemed to do in taking over Oswald was to make him a forerunner of Disney's other great character (other than Mickey, that is), Donald Duck: to be feisty, temperamental, quick to be irritated and, if anything, prone to be unlucky rather than lucky.

Indeed, Harman's *Sick Cylinders*, a title the Disneys would never have come up with, is a trial run for a classic Technicolor Duck, *Don Donald* of 1936. In each the little fellow, Oswald or Donald, jumps into his jaunty anthropomorphic open roadster to take a sweetie for a ride. (In *Don Donald* she is Dona, later known as Daisy.) There are mechanical troubles. So the ride is anything but smooth, much to the lady's displeasure. In both cartoons the vexed driver and his opponent, the car, are the main characters.

Better yet is Rudy Ising's *Homeless Homer*, with help from Friz Freleng. This is a remarkable effort with phenomenal inventive touches.

On a snowy day, Oswald invites a teeny rabbit, maybe a nephew, in for roast turkey or chicken and trimmings. Kid grabs the whole carcass. No, no. A baby's milk bottle for him. Which the kid rejects by squirting Oswald and so on. Peas and potatoes are to be eaten politely with fork, not a knife. The kid retaliates—a mess ensues, a bath is in order.

While sitting in the washtub, the kid manages to tie Oswald's head onto the cord of a window-shade, resulting in head flying off his body as a balloon. We are now far from logic. The wee rascal, unknown to his host, ties an endless rope onto him and stretches it through the house, over a transom, finally attaching it

Looney Tunes & Happy Harmonies 211

Rudy Ising: *Homless Homer* (1928)

to a player-piano. When the piano roll rolls, the rope pulls Oswald in a zigzag, dizzying course quickly this way and that. All done with brilliant animation, a feast for the eye.

It's a bravura extended moment. *Homeless Homer* is one of the top silent cartoons, on par with the best of Felix or Fleischer. So what Harman and Ising might have done if Oswald was left in their hands we can only guess.

Soon, Oswald was under the guidance of Walter Lantz and, while there were a few good *Oswalds* ahead, such as *Annie Moved Away* (1934) and *Night Life of the Bugs* (1936), Oswald became fluffy and cuddly and white instead of inky black and spontaneous.

After the stint with Mintz, Hugh Harman invented a new character, Bosko. Bosko wore clothes and was not quite a young man or boy, nor was he a monkey without a tail. Alas, he did have a habit of calling out, "Mammy!" Bosko had a signature move—to stretch out one leg, then slide it in the Bosko shuffle.

In 1930 Leon Schlesinger hired the team to start the first animation set-up at Warner Bros. Friz Freleng came along. Bosko was the star. Like Mickey, Bosko had a girlfriend. Her name, Honey. And a pet dog, Bruno. If Uncle Walt had *Silly Symphonies*, Harman-Ising, with tongue in cheek, had *Looney Tunes*. And in 1931, an added touch of whimsy, *Merrie Melodies*. Now they were joined by Bob Clampett. A further poking fun at Disney was, slyly, in a blink of an eye, to have a Mickey lookalike race through the back of a scene. Lantz and other animators of the early Thirties saluted the famed Mouse in like manner.

It was obvious that Mickey Mouse got better and better. He became a courageous fellow, forever cheerful, adventurous, fun to be around. He ventured into Darkest Africa, escaping from a cannibal stewpot in *Trader Mickey* (1932); was a fairytale hero in *Ye Olden Days* and confronted King Kong in *The Pet Shop* (both 1933).

Composed entirely of circles, Mickey was design-friendly. Bosko (like Ubbe Iwerks' froggy answer to Mickey, Flip) was not nearly so appealing. Most Boskos find him dancing at any opportunity along with flowers or anything handy. Music is the glue that holds him together; this follows the pattern of early Mickeys. All are short on plot. But Mickey took chances.

So did Bosko, a bit lamely—dreaming he was a knight in the era of King Arthur in *Bosko's Knight-Mare* (1933); a Legionnaire in *Beau Bosko* and a Musketeer in *Bosko the Musketeer* (both 1933).

However, one of the most significant Boskos is 1931's *Bosko the Doughboy*, where cannons shoot wildly at unmanned cannons in impressive numbers. In the midst of death and carnage, Bosko is in a dugout dining on a can of beans—oblivious to a world at war. His buddy is a roly-poly hippo soldier. Bombs are dropped by a pelican that gets shot down. The hippo is killed. Bosko, unfazed, shouts, "I'll save you, pal!" This is a cartoon—after all. He unzips the hippo's belly and removes a cannonball. "Mammy!"

Hugh Harman's design for *Bosko* (1928-9)

Bosko in *The Tree's Knees* (1931)

At decade's close, Hugh Harman was to develop the war theme in his *Peace on Earth*, unforgettably.

And he would not give up on Bosko either.

Meanwhile, Rudy Ising (and presumably Clampett) was attending to *Merrie Melodies* with greater success. For one, Harman-Ising had full use of the music library owned by Warner Bros., gratis, often striking pay dirt. For instance, *The Organ Grinder* from 1933 is a dandy, energetic cartoon blessed by having a loveable monkey, Tony, who scurries along in a tenement setting with his tin cup. Tony is wonderfully drawn, cute as a button.

The monkey dons a wig as Harpo Marx; he also impersonates both Laurel *and* Hardy. He plays two pianos—one with his paws, one with his feet—and becomes a one-man band, including concertina and drums, doing "42nd Street." Ever busy, Tony drives an auto (an odd touch: a brassiere covers the headlights), which crashes into a fruit stand and a music store.

Too bad this was a one-shot cartoon. Tony has more spirit than Goopy Gear of *Foxy* or Bosko. Combined.

And there's the stupendous *A Great Big Bunch of You* (1932) and *The Dish Ran Away with the Spoon* (1933). *A Great Big Bunch of You* takes place at the City Dump where all sorts of items are tossed, including a grandfatherly clock, shoes, toy soldiers, a hat rack, bottles and several mannequins, and these come to life to sing and dance in a most infectious manner and, at the close, one mannequin pops out of the garbage to ask Ted Lewis's famous question, "Is Everybody Happy?"

Altogether, a nifty confection.

Virtually Ising's swansong at WB is *The Dish Ran Away with the Spoon*. Utensils, pots, plates, a colander and more cavort musically with manic gusto as Mister Spoon falls head over heels for Miss Dish (saved from a monster made from cookie dough). This one is a nonstop irresistible delight with, as Jerry Beck has pointed out, Ising giving objects uses they would never have otherwise. It's a device to be used later by Harman-Ising, particularly wonderfully in the amazing *Bottles* (1936) and *Pipe Dream* (1938).

More than once, Hugh Harman especially was to run afoul of budget constraints. Since Leon Schlesinger was wont to cut the budget rather than to allow more money, Harman and Ising were obliged in 1933 to say, "So long, folks!" And move on.

A temporary haven was found with Amedee Van Beuren, whose black-and-white cartoons were released through RKO. They were to finish two *Cubby Bear* cartoons that same year; in essence, elaborate Boskos. In *The Gay Gaucho,* Cubby has Bosko expressions and characteristics. Including the trademark Bosko shuffle. A South of the Border theme was to be a future Ising favorite.

Cubby Bear's World Flight is a busy reel populated with well-known personalities: the Marx Brothers, "Lindy" himself (Cubby's plane is "The Spirit of Ammonia"), Hitler (already in 1933!), Maurice Chevalier and the Devil. Cubby's aircraft spins down through the entire planet—coming out of course in China. *World Flight* has a spectacularly animated sea storm with giant rolling waves and bolts of lightning as nice as Ubbe Iwerks' *Flip* cartoon, *Stormy Seas,* made the year before.

The boys aimed for something higher than Amedee Van Beuren and they got it: the privilege of opening a set-up at MGM, which had only minor success in distributing Iwerks' work, the Flips, the Willie Whoppers and Fairytales cartoons.

They brought Hugh Harman's Bosko in too and, hooray, had use of color. Disney had exclusive dibs on Technicolor. So at first the energized team was limited to a two-strip process that Ising used beautifully in *The Calico Dragon* and *The Chinese Nightingale* (both 1935). To be fair, Iwerks employed Cinecolor to glorious effect in *Jack Frost, The Headless Horseman* and *Don Quixote* in 1934.

In such films, honestly, you seldom notice any colors left out. I fail to see how even the full spectrum would improve *The Calico Dragon* in which the counterpane on a little girl's bed becomes the landscape for adventures of a toy horse and knight-errant. At Warners, they had Frank Marsales to add music to their labors; at MGM they had one of the best, Scott Bradley, who wrote for them many memorable scores. And another playful jab at Walter Elias Disney: they became *Happy Harmonies*. So there!

They were never to have a *Three Little Pigs* or a *Band Concert*, a *Ferdinand the Bull* or *Ugly Duckling*. Yet, they were to think up equally masterful, more unusual one-reelers: *Bottles* (1936), *To Spring* (also 1936) and *Swing Wedding* (1937) with Hugh Harman at the helm. These are cartoons I would die for. Harman is my man, for he had the blessed inspiration to make Bosko a bona-fide little black boy, the most lovable child in cartoonland.

In three titles, *Bosko and the Pirates* (1937), *Bosko and the Cannibals* (also 1937) and *Bosko in Bagdad* (1938), Bosko sets out innocently with a sack of cookies, declaring, "Off to Gran'ma's here ah go!" and each time encounters a group of frogs who excitedly shout, "*He's got the cookies! We ain't got cookies!*" The giant frogs, disguised as pirates, cannibals or Bagdadians, connive to take the treasure from his grasp.

These all-new Boskos are deliriously upbeat. The color magnificent, the pacing sensational. The cast includes frogs in the form of Louis Armstrong, Bill Robinson, Fats Waller, the Ink Spots and Cab Calloway. The tempo grows wilder and most frenzied with Bosko dancing up a storm. In the end, he outwits them and the cookies are saved.

What Harman or Ising did not guess (nor did Hungarian George Pal with his tuneful Puppetoons starring Jasper) was that it might be thought incorrect for a white man to make a "black" cartoon—even if in homage to great musicians and entertainers.

Bosko in Bagdad raises the Boskos to such a level of perfection there was nowhere to go. Goodbye, Bosko, just as after Mickey

Hugh Harman: *Bosko in Bagdad* (1938)

Hugh Harman: *Bosko in Bagdad* (1938)

became the "Sorcerer's Apprentice," what should Mickey do? Leave on a high note.

If you have never viewed the "Mona Lisa," I find it impossible to convey adequately in words what the painting does. My theory is it's the eyes that engage you, lock you in, not the half-smile on her lips. Better for you to experience what Da Vinci wrought in person. Likewise, Hugh Harman's *Bottles*. I can try to describe it, but what it does and how it does it is beyond words. On a rainy night at an apothecary shop, the elderly proprietor dozes among vials and tubes and ointments and bottles of all kinds. Suddenly, a poison bottle ominously shrieks, "Death walks the night!" And with a few drops on the druggist's head, shrinks him and he wakes up finding himself no bigger than bottles on his shelves.

"Well, bless my soul!" he says and an India-ink bottle lures a tube of ointment to squeeze a snake shape out to wriggle, the cold cream tries to warm itself unsuccessfully by a fire, the witch hazel cackles shrilly, spirits of ammonia warn of "things that creep upon ya," and the poison traps the old man inside glass tubes containing bright liquids. The druggist awakens to repeat, "Bless my soul!"

In a different mode is *To Spring*, another Harman extravaganza—in which Hobbit-size creatures, little brown men who sleep underground all winter, stretch and yawn and prepare the vivid colors that Spring brings to the earth. Technicolor is explored to the max, just as the live-action short *La Cucaracha* did in 1934 and Mamoulian did in the 1935 feature *Becky Sharp*. Uncle Walt detested *To Spring*; at a story conference on *Snow White* in 1936, he told his staff the color was outrageous. Much too strong. *To Spring* is a lyrical masterpiece.

Hugh Harman: *Peace On Earth* (1939)

And *Swing Wedding* in 1937 is another excursion into frog country with a lady fish the spitting image of Ethel Waters; lest we forget, Miss Waters was once young and sexy and rather bawdy. The orchestra leader, of course, is a Cab Calloway figure, and the groom a Stepin Fetchit. Sadly maligned today, Fetchit was a brilliant comic, adored once by African Americans for whom he originated an act as a sleepy, sly, slow-moving fellow. Louis Armstrong and Flip Wilson were among his steadfast supporters.

Swing Wedding, like the three Boskos, builds and builds to a heady, noisy crescendo and more than hints at heroin addiction; at the finish, musicians smash their instruments. Nothing new under the sun, eh? On a roll, Harman also gave MGM its money's worth with *Pipe Dreams* (released early 1938).

Midnight; logs burn on a hearth; on the mantelpiece sit statues of monkeys See No Evil, Hear No Evil, Speak No Evil, who stuff a pipe with Helz Fire smoking tobacco and inhale deeply. Lying in an ashtray are hobo cigars who comment, "What's so good about being *good*? What's so bad about being *bad*?" All hop aboard a train made of matchboxes. A corncob-pipe band plays; Mexican cigars dance. Pipe-stem cleaner bandits chase the monkeys back to the mantel and home.

In late 1937, MGM took the boys to court. Money, money, money. Delay on contracted-for cartoons. In their absence, Friz Freleng was to produce *Captain and the Kids* specials, most of them in sepia. *The Good Earth* looked dandy that way and so would *Tortilla Flat*. But the lackluster Frelengs were cost-cutters and no more related to the comic strip than the *Krazy Kats* at Columbia were to Herriman's iconoclastic originals.

To Harman-Ising's rescue came Walt Disney, who needed more product to be released through RKO. The result was a superior *Silly Symphony*, *Merbabies*, a visual gem that runs circles around the Disney *Water Babies* of 1935. It's one of the finest *Sillies* and surely had an influence on the underwater scenes in *Pinocchio*.

The lawsuit settled, the boys, like the proverbial cat, came back, this time in a new arrangement. The title card would no longer read "Harman-Ising." Instead, it would read "A Hugh Harman Production" or "A Rudolf Ising Production."

Bosko was gone, nevertheless Harman had fresh ideas. He would demonstrate his interest in higher matters with *The Art Gallery* and *The Bookworm* (both 1939); he ended the year with *The Mad Maestro* and *Peace on Earth*. If he were remembered for one cartoon, it would be the latter. He was the one animator who took notice of Poland and Czechoslovakia. On Christmas Eve, Grandpa Squirrel relates how the last men on Earth fought to the death. Grandpa thinks it was the vegetarians against the meat-eaters, the flat-footed people against the buck-toothed people. The animals survived to "rebuild the old wastes," making houses from the iron helmets of the soldiers. It's a harrowing fable; the battle scenes are drawn with serious realism.

Hugh Harman was the temperamental one. Rudy Ising, whose character was more laidback, offered Barney Bear who, it was said, was basically himself disguised, very sweet-natured, calm and placid. The *Barney Bear* series continued long after Harman and Ising left MGM. And *The Dance of the Weed* was his triumphant 1941 charmer, proof that he could produce what is, in essence, the last *Silly Symphony*.

When the boys arrived at MGM in 1934, they brought their own composer, Scott Bradley. The creative variety of their cartoons gave him free rein to write music for what he called "fantasies," to give them "significance," to be "musically sound and entertaining." *The Dance of the Weed* was to give him his best chance. For this one he composed the music first—a veritable symphonic poem. As Bradley mentioned in a speech at the Film Music Forum years later, it was intended as a ballet for flowers. A bashful, homely weed (the boy) and a pretty ballerina wild-rose (the girl) tentatively fall in love; she is menaced by a nasty three-headed snapdragon; the weed foils the snapdragon and together they escape across a lyrical enchanted landscape, joyously.

Bradley was proud of his score for *The Dance of the Weed*, justifiably, and reworked it into a concert piece.

Rudy Ising: *Dance of the Weed* (1941)

Model sheet for Rudy Ising cartoon later titled
Little Gravel Voice (1942)

With WWII, there came radical changes at MGM; artiness was out. Garbo, Luise Rainer were out; Conrad Veidt was loaned to Columbia and Warner Bros. June Allyson and Van Johnson were in and Judy Garland remained. Hugh Harman and Rudy Ising were out. Tex Avery was in while Hanna-Barbera, who worked under the boys, remained.

The world is loaded with irony, then and now. It's been told that Hugh Harman in 1925 doodled mice on a photo of Walt Disney; these inspired Ubbe Iwerks who, in 1928, drew the first Mickeys. In 1939, Rudy Ising produced a cartoon, *Puss Gets the Boot*, the tale of a mouse named Jerry and a cat named Jasper.

Youngsters Bill Hanna and Joe Barbera contributed to this cartoon. Literally, soon Ising (and Harman) got the boot, again for cost overruns. Hanna-Barbera got stuck in a squirrel cage with what became *Tom and Jerry* for twenty prosperous years. There were (by my count) 109 Hanna-Barbera *Tom and Jerrys*. Scott Bradley stayed on to write for them what he called the necessary "violent music." From the moguls' point of view, Harman and Ising paid scant attention to budget. Their cartoons often fill up a full reel. Hanna-Barbera's would run two-thirds of a reel, following a recipe using the same ingredients, ad nauseum.

Chuck Jones's *Road Runner* series at WB (a modest 22 only) in the Fifties and Sixties used a similar formula—in his case more like sticking to the rules of a sonnet or a haiku—with greater wit, color and graphic design. Chuck Jones also gave us *Tom Thumb in Trouble*, Sniffles, *One Froggy Evening, Duck Dodgers in the 24½th Century, What's Opera Doc?* and *Drip-Along Daffy*.

He's in another league altogether.

In a short span of six years (1934-41, allowing for the year away, 1938) the collective art of Hugh Harman and Rudy Ising developed continually. They did astounding, timeless and eye-catching one-reelers while the Fleischers and the Disneys tooled up for features. *Snow White, Pinocchio, Gulliver's Travels* and *Mr. Bug Goes to Town* are something to behold; however, if Harman-Ising had been able to adapt, say, T.E. White's Arthurian tome, *The Once and Future King*, then we might have reached the Holy Grail of animation.

I have found the right combination of Harman-Ising magic can make you high, whatever that means. Show a half dozen of these and the audience comes out lightheaded and awestruck. A giddy pleasure.

Both men got employed by the military during the war; Ising as a captain. Did they make cartoons such as the *Private Snafu* ones? I forgot to ask Mr. Ising when I spoke to him some thirty years ago. After the war it seems they worked catch as catch can in industrial and TV advertising. Harman held onto his dream of attempting a King Arthur feature but the compromise was disappointing definitely. With Gordon Sheehan he made *Tom Thumb in King Arthur's Court* in 16mm Kodachrome for Coronet Films in Chicago. This dismal, quite clumsy two-reeler took five years to complete (1949 to 1953) owing to Harman's drinking problem.

On the other hand, my friend June Jollie Brown, a former *Vogue* model and wife of writer Harry Brown, said, imbibing or not, he was fantastically light on his feet. Ladies remember things like that.

Much superior was the three-reel *Easy Does It* made by Hugh Harman for Stokeley Van Camp in 1946 (in 16mm Kodachrome) under the proud banner of "Hugh Harman Productions."

After Laugh-O-Grams failed, Harman and Ising briefly had their own company, Arabian Nights Cartoons in 1923, the closest they came to being independent.

(Russell Merritt collection)

A buddy of mine is a well-known collector and producer for video and DVD of significant film classics; he lived for awhile in Laurel Canyon. When I visited him, this pal, who knew of my regard for the works of H & I, walked his dog each morning after breakfast. He insisted I stay at the house while he did so—asking me to answer the telephone if it rang. On the day I left, with a twinkle in his eye, he revealed that every day he encountered Hugh Harman walking *his* dog at the same hour.

Thus, I was deprived of meeting the animator I would have cherished most meeting. My pal's little joke and my grievous loss.

I did have the pleasure of talking with my other hero, Rudy Ising, and we exchanged letters. In one, I was thrilled to learn he had put my book, *Jeremiah Knucklebones*, which I dedicated to him, under the Christmas tree for the Ising grandkids. The precious letters lay in a leather valise, my traveling office during my years in Mexico. Robbers who broke into my house elected to burn the valise and its contents for it contained nothing of value to them.

But I have the memory of my book resting beneath Rudolf Ising's Christmas tree.

Chapter 15
Glamour-Pusses Up Close:
Mae West, Marlene Dietrich, Dolores Del Rio, and Rita Hayworth

Illusion makes life tolerable. We once thought F.D.R. could walk; Hepburn and Tracy, Kelly and Rainier, Charles and Diana were storybook couples. If only it were so! How good we felt, believing. No place did it better, this business of illusion-making, than Hollywood in its prime. Hortense Powdermaker called it the "Dream Factory."

According to set designers Cedric Gibbons and Charles D. Hall, in grand houses windows and curtains stretched to the sky and beyond and the ceilings were higher than that. According to makeup artist Max Factor, all stars had flawless complexions. If one of them had a mole (Joan Blondell, Ginger Rogers), it was a beauty mark to envy. According to dress designers Gilbert Adrian or Edith Head, just about every leading lady displayed a perfect figure.

Life might be tough outside the movie palaces; however, step aside, throw cares away and admire the glorious creatures that were not the girls next door. They had help. Marlene required a lot of artifice...her famous key-light, the sucked-in cheeks, the weird eyebrows plucked just so. Garbo needed very little, after MGM assisted Mother Nature a bit...she lost weight, her teeth got straightened. Garbo's luscious long lashes were real.

Lucky me, I encountered a handful of these incredible women, the likes of which we are never to see again. Today, we live in Barbie Doll time with few exceptions. The following stars are one-of-a-kind.

MAE WEST

The reviewer for stage and screen on *The Toledo Times* was a kindly person named Ruth Elgutter. If a special celebrity came to town she telephoned and I hopped on an Old Orchard bus to meet Miss Elgutter at the Town Hall Theater. She'd take me into the dressing room where I stood in a corner to listen and observe. In this way I met Tallulah Bankhead and Mae West. Miss West was there for *Catherine Was Great*. Years before, she almost did it as a Technicolor feature at Paramount. Next morning in the column, Ruth Elgutter declared that the star did not swear or smoke or drink. Throughout the interview, Miss West, ample of bosom, quite short of stature and who wore lifts in her shoes, smoked a pink cigarette in a bejeweled holder. She sat at the dressing-table—suddenly turned and saw me, an eleven-year-old kid, snapping, "Get that little shit out of here." I wonder if she drank. How discreet newspaper people were then.

Mae West invented herself, decided she must be the sexiest creature alive and kept that notion as long as she lived. At age sixty-seven she wrote a play for herself called *Sextette*. It came

Mae West, 1936 (Marty Kearns collection)

to Detroit. So I hopped on the Greyhound. Nothing could stop me. There was lots of West wit still...rather, since she had great timing she made it sound witty. "What is marriage?" she sighed. "Letting one man make love to you at a time." Not so hilarious on the page but out of her rosebud mouth it was. "Beulah, peel me a grape," is not Wilde-ian. However, I'll bet she could make Oscar Wilde uneasy.

Mae West, 19??

Jack LaRue, one of her co-stars, died the night before onstage. Yet that didn't stop Miss West, although I detected a bit of gloom over the others. After the play I hurried backstage to meet her. An oxygen tank was artfully half-hidden. A stagehand said every time Miss West walked that walk out of the scene, she took a deep whiff to get her through the next minutes. What a trouper!

I saw that she had the most flawless skin—pale white silk like a baby's behind. It positively glowed. She claimed no ordinary soap ever touched her; she only used face cream.

At age eighty-five she was to turn *Sextette* into her last feature. And guess who were the six vying for her dimpled hand? Timothy Dalton (a.k.a. James Bond), Ringo Starr, Walter Pidgeon, George Hamilton, Tony Curtis and George Raft. What a woman!

MARLENE DIETRICH

Not enough tickets were sold for Marlene when she was to appear in Toledo; the show got cancelled. Happily, I was in Copenhagen when she was to be at Tivoli Gardens concert hall with Burt Bachrach and his orchestra early in the Seventies. Copenhagen was all a-twitter. Europe often takes a longer view; Zizi Jeanmaire and Josephine Baker had faithful followers to the end of their careers.

Don Loper (from Toledo) fifteen years earlier had designed a fabulous latex bodysuit that La Dietrich wore in Las Vegas, astonishing the beholders. The lady had lost so much flesh over time; she was not as lushly curvy as she's been in *The Blue Angel* when she tipped the scales at 175. Don Loper to the rescue!

Remember Groucho Marx's line: "Who are you going to believe—me or your own eyes?" I witnessed the international charmer Merle Oberon at her home in Acapulco. She was in her late sixties and yet wore a revealing bikini, exhibiting a phenomenal figure. She really did.

That night, in Copenhagen, following the performance, Marlene, at dinner, no longer hid under pink and blue lights; no

Marlene Dietrich (1930) by Josef von Sternberg with his favorite top keylight

key-light above to accentuate the cheekbones. She was a living mannequin. Hands and neck ancient; her face a Kabuki mask.

At Tivoli she was a ghost of herself. In trademark world-weary style, she dragged a rabbit wrap across the stage. It was supposed to be chinchilla. Where the performance came alive was when she sang the anti-war song "Where Have All the Flowers Gone?" Suddenly, she sang with a kind of passionate conviction, wowing the audience. You felt a jolt of electricity.

There was another high point, unforgettable. The first twenty minutes of her program the third row was strangely empty. I sat

Marlene Dietrich, 19??

in row four. Then came clattering down the aisle, on unsteady high heels, two dozen transvestites of diverse ages and weight, Marlene look-alikes. They looked more like Marlene than she did. It was phenomenal. She was displeased, to put it mildly.

Soon after gala concerts in London, Stockholm and Paris, Marlene Dietrich the indestructible disappeared from view, locking herself in her Paris flat, not wishing to be seen ever again.

Perhaps she looked in the mirror too many times. In Berlin a few years ago, I got permission to go to the huge warehouse where her belongings are stored. She kept everything. If there was an excellent signed photo by Hurrell, she had ten of them. She must have walked away with every frock she wore. Every diamond-studded cigarette case. Every doodad. Every pair of shoes.

I searched for the shoes she takes off at the close of *Morocco* as she follows Gary Cooper and the Foreign Legion over the sands of the Sahara. I'm sure they are there somewhere in a climate-controlled vault. Where they will never age.

DOLORES DEL RIO

Just whom did the camera love best? I nominate Greta Garbo and Dolores Del Rio. This is not to forget Silvana Mangano and Hedy Lamarr or another Dolores (Costello). The camera eye is mesmerized by these ladies. Whether they moved or stood in repose doesn't matter; they are the centers of attention. Almost anybody else can be in the same shot—tough luck.

Garbo exudes a magic essence, so does Del Rio, and they were born to be photographed and the proof of it will last as long as motion picture film is preserved. Of course, nothing beats seeing them in pristine nitrate glory.

Dolores Del Rio, from Durango, Mexico, was a cousin to another gorgeous star, Ramon Navarro. Like him, she was part of the first Mexican wave in Hollywood along with Lupe Velez and Gilbert Roland. Her part as Charmaine, a French girl pur-

Dolores Del Rio, 1937 (Marty Kearns collection)

sued by doughboys Victor McLaglen and Edmund Lowe, in *What Price Glory?* (1926) did not go unnoticed. She had star billing in Edwin Carewe's *Evangeline* (1929). In the Thirties she bewitched audiences as a Polynesian in *Bird of Paradise* (1932), opposite Joel McCrea, and again most fetchingly French in *Madame DuBarry* (1934). Married to Cedric Gibbons, she was pretty much ornamental the rest of that decade. In the Forties, divorcing Gibbons, she nearly married Orson Welles and was lovely in his production of the elegant thriller *Journey into Fear* (1942).

Wisely, she made a return to her native land, where the great Emilio Fernandez let her show her full range in a superb tragic drama, *Maria Candelaria*. At last she had a cameraman worthy of her (as Garbo did in William Daniels), Gabriel Figueroa, and this unbeatable team won the Grand Prize at Cannes in 1946. Now John Ford wanted her (and Figueroa) for *The Fugitive* in 1947; the co-star was Henry Fonda as a runaway priest she protects. During the Fifties she shared her talents on stage and screen. In 1960 she became Elvis Presley's American-Indian mother in *Flaming Star*. Her last film was 1978's *The Children of Sanchez* with Anthony Quinn. She played a fetching prostitute.

This is more or less where I come in, for Dolores Del Rio became the patroness of the Cervantes Festival held in Guanajuato. At the beginning, it was only the one-act plays by Miguel Cervantes at the University in an open square (okay, a circle shape). It grew into a yearly arts celebration with puppet plays from Poland, dancers from the States, an international affair.

I had a house in nearby Marfil, made from the ruins of a silver mining refinery from the 1600s; this was in the gray-brown mountains of central Mexico, eight thousand feet up. An architect from

Dolores Del Rio, 19??

Venice, Giorgio Belloli, ingeniously transformed these old ruins into fantastic homes with exotic gardens, bougainvillea and jacaranda, lime and avocado trees.

Would I be willing to have a party for Miss Del Rio in my garden? Si, si. That night as the round, red sun slipped past the mountains of Guanajuato, an orange moon lit up the sky. Below, I lit two hundred candles. Thick scent of bougainvillea and various fruits hung in the air. Partygoers gathered, sangria in hand.

Then she appeared. Wearing a silk floor-length skirt with pastel rosebuds, she flew, not ran, down the twenty-some stone steps into the garden. The crowd gasped. She seemed a young creature of thirty-five.

Time passes.

An art opening was held in a former convent in Patzcuaro on Lake Patzcuaro in the state of Michuacan, a place always green because of constant rain. The Conquistadors built the town in the 1500s; the roofs are red-tiled like in northern Italy.

I came with my amigo Isaac who wore an elaborate outfit such as Gustav Klimt might have worn. The gallery's floor was made from cow hooves. Isaac greeted his admirers and backed into the room. All at once from the opposite corner Dolores Del Rio also backed in, acknowledging fans. The gallery itself was empty. Oh oh. They collided at its center and fell plop onto a cow hoof floor. Couldn't be comfortable. As she lay there, she recognized Isaac...both stayed prone, laughing, holding a conversation. I was impressed. She thought it funny.

Time passes.

Miss Del Rio did *Camille* in Mexico City. Didn't want to miss that. I took a Yellow Arrow bus (Flecha Amarilla). The motto of that line is "Better Dead Than Late." Everybody in the cast was older than usual (shades of Mae West). Armand, Marguerite's lover, was forty-ish with graying sideburns. Dolores Del Rio looked thirty-five sneaking up on forty. This was her second performance of the day.

Dolores Del Rio, 19??

Venice, Giorgio Belloli, ingeniously transformed these old ruins into fantastic homes with exotic gardens, bougainvillea and jacaranda, lime and avocado trees.

Would I be willing to have a party for Miss Del Rio in my garden? Si, si. That night as the round, red sun slipped past the mountains of Guanajuato, an orange moon lit up the sky. Below, I lit two hundred candles. Thick scent of bougainvillea and various fruits hung in the air. Partygoers gathered, sangria in hand.

Then she appeared. Wearing a silk floor-length skirt with pastel rosebuds, she flew, not ran, down the twenty-some stone steps into the garden. The crowd gasped. She seemed a young creature of thirty-five.

Time passes.

An art opening was held in a former convent in Patzcuaro on Lake Patzcuaro in the state of Michuacan, a place always green because of constant rain. The Conquistadors built the town in the 1500s; the roofs are red-tiled like in northern Italy.

I came with my amigo Isaac who wore an elaborate outfit such as Gustav Klimt might have worn. The gallery's floor was made from cow hooves. Isaac greeted his admirers and backed into the room. All at once from the opposite corner Dolores Del Rio also backed in, acknowledging fans. The gallery itself was empty. Oh oh. They collided at its center and fell plop onto a cow hoof floor. Couldn't be comfortable. As she lay there, she recognized Isaac… both stayed prone, laughing, holding a conversation. I was impressed. She thought it funny.

Time passes.

Miss Del Rio did *Camille* in Mexico City. Didn't want to miss that. I took a Yellow Arrow bus (Flecha Amarilla). The motto of that line is "Better Dead Than Late." Everybody in the cast was older than usual (shades of Mae West). Armand, Marguerite's lover, was forty-ish with graying sideburns. Dolores Del Rio looked thirty-five sneaking up on forty. This was her second performance of the day.

At the end, Marguerite expired on the chaise, dropping her flower. All the lights went out except for a small shimmering spot on the white camellia. Next, that light was extinguished, too. The curtains closed. When they reopened for the curtain calls, of which there were many, every ounce of energy got drained from the star. At that moment, and only then, she was seventy-five.

RITA HAYWORTH

In Mexico, I lived down the lane from Harry Brown, poet, novelist, screenwriter of note; he wrote the first *Ocean's Eleven*. His classic WWII novel *A Walk in the Sun* became an equally classic film directed by Lewis Milestone. His novel *The Stars in Their Courses* was made into *El Dorado* with Robert Mitchum and John Wayne. Harry's voluptuous wife June had been a model and actress; Richard Avedon photographed her for the cover of *Paris Vogue*. Her seasoned beauty caused students at the University to whisper, if we went to market, "Mrs. Robinson?" She pretended to be displeased.

Other gringo neighbors, in casas Signor Belloli built from the silver refinery's ruins, were Fletcher Martin, distinguished painter, print-maker; his wife, Jean, who was "Houseboat Hannah" on the radio soap opera; Elsa Clay, secretary to composer Bernard Herrmann (*Citizen Kane, Fahrenheit 451, The Day the Earth Stood Still*); Gilbert and Lydia Hunt of the Texas railroad dynasty; Garth Williams, illustrator of *Charlotte's Web* and *Stuart Little*; Conrad Woods, son of Donald Woods, a Warner Bros. second-tier leading man of the 1930s; Bill Overgard, artist for the comic strip *Steve Canyon*; and a Canadian pornographer who wrote under the name Chastity Bell.

Rita Hayworth (1942)

A motley, talented bunch. My initial visit to Marfil was to light a candle under Garth Williams, who invented a motto "No Work Between Meals." He had been signed by Harper to illustrate one of my books, *Push Kitty*. I fell in love with the place and June Brown, who acted as rental and sales agent, told me one of the nicest homes was available. The owners had been accused of something and they fled in their pajamas. The wife left Coco Chanel tweed suits in the closet; they were worn by the maids, Chona and Paula. My own impression is that surrealism was born in Mexico, not France.

Burt Lancaster came to my gate one morning; he meant to visit Harry Brown. I invited him to come for breakfast next morning. And Burt came. A marvelous meal—eggs rancheros on fresh tortillas, orange juice just squeezed from oranges in the garden, but no coffee. I had a swell English silver coffee urn which Broderick Crawford gave me. I'd helped him buy some English silver in Demark. I took Chona aside, congratulating her on her tasty eggs rancheros. Why no coffee? "The coffee pot committed suicide," she said with a very sober face. I don't recall what I told Burt Lancaster.

Rita Hayworth in The Wrath of God, 1972
(Michael Holo collection)

The year is 1972. MGM was to do location work on *The Wrath of God*, to star Robert Mitchum as a gun-running American padre, Frank Langella was to play Dolores Del Rio's son. It turned out Miss Del Rio did not take the role—she already played mother to Elvis; couldn't top it. Rita Hayworth replaced her. Locations were to be in the state of Querétero where MGM promised the villagers of La Mina, a defunct mining place (the Japanese had removed all its opals), that they would rebuild the village and, most importantly, the run-down church. They did not. They made facades that they tore down when they left.

Harry Brown was asked to improvise dialog, but wasn't in shape for it. So his enterprising spouse, gorgeous June, volunteered me. Me? I write about rabbits on roller skates. I'll give it a try, I declared gamely.

I met Mitchum first, an easygoing laidback guy. To my delight, he admitted he wrote poetry and when a lad of twenty or so had written puppet plays. More of him later. When Langella leaped in the sole Cadillac to get to the location shoot, leaving icon Rita Hayworth to ride in a rattletrap truck, I was astonished.

Miss Hayworth was a puzzle to us. She looked wonderful and mostly wore tight-fitting outfits. Her figure and face were fantastic. But the mind drifted elsewhere. Each day she only learned a few lines. We assumed it was from years of imbibing or smoking, results of a high life with Aly Khan and Orson Welles, The carotid clogged artery thing. Alzheimer's was then not yet part of our vocabulary.

What was my task exactly? Pretty silly. In one scene Mitchum, in priest's robes, ran out from the church, stumbling on a large stone. "What do I say here?" he asked. "What about 'Goddamit

Robert Mitchum and Rita Hayworth on location in Mexico, 1972 (Michael Holo collection)

to Hell!'" I offered. "Great!" said Mitchum. Not high art exactly. When not on camera, Miss Hayworth kept to herself. Little did we guess how much she was suffering. She resembled Gilda in delectable middle age, but the fire had gone out.

One evening, Mitchum and I had dinner at the Canadian pornographer's; they lived uphill on "poor street" (no cobblestones, just dirt). In the middle of flan, the dessert, we heard tinkling of the bells. Boys were bringing goats down the mountain. Mitchum's eyes twinkled with mischief.

He rushed out of the little house and in a minute returned with a burro which he led onto the Chinese carpet. "Here's a parlor trick I learned from John Huston in Ireland," he said. And he proceeded to masturbate the animal. The evening broke up. We didn't shake hands.

Miss Hayworth's location scenes over, she prepared to return to Beverly Hills where her daughter Yasmine was to take care of her, according to my late friend, the vivacious Andrea King. During a three-hour trip to Mexico City, Miss Hayworth said nothing. I kept chattering away and she would respond with a giggle or nod of the head. I deposited her at the Camino Real. We would meet at six o'clock.

We had a few marguerites at the hotel and then went to the Pink Zone to Bellinghausen, a classy German restaurant where a trio of elderly Germans played Viennese waltzes as we dined. My amigo Isaac ordered for Miss Hayworth and me; I was busy keeping her entertained. Drinks were flowing. The main course arrived. It was a good-sized fish totally encrusted on two sides with toasted almonds. More drinks. It got easier and easier to amuse the lady.

Toasted almonds warmed our happy insides. It turned out they were tasty cloves of garlic—not almonds. We had digested hundreds of them. Then it happened. I heard Miss Hayworth fart, a quiet one. But definitely a fart. The erotic goddess, Gilda, doing that? Isaac moved his chair away from the table at a safe distance as a duel ensued.

I could perform better ones. Loud or squeaky. And Rita improved upon mine. We tried doing Morse code. Now green fumes surrounded our table. We laughed heartily, pumped up by our expertise. Finally, a haughty waiter guided us to the door without presenting a bill.

Isaac, who arranged the whole spectacle, observed without comment. I put her in a taxi; she roared with merriment. The taxi pulled away. And that is the last I saw of Rita Hayworth.

Chapter 16
How I Became America's Best Otter

A small boy from Circleville, Ohio, wrote me: "You are a good otter. You are America's best otter." This is encouraging. Somebody likes my work. Notice the leap of faith from "good" to "America's best." The spelling is charming.

What to be when you grow up? That is the question. I was trained for eleven years to be a musician, not a writer of children's books. As a kid I once turned the pages for Leonard Bernstein when he visited my teacher, Elizabeth Gould. Also, as a kid magician, I appeared onstage with Harry Blackstone himself. So how did I turn out to be neither *musician* nor *magician*?

At seventeen, I had a chance to understudy with Max Steiner; my dream: to be a film composer. My idols: Erich Korngold and Franz Waxman. My own music tended to be light Viennese Operetta. But a new kind of movie music was underfoot—Leonard Rosenman, for example, who scored *East of Eden* and *Rebel Without a Cause*. Less symphonic. To my tender ear, tortured jazz.

Off I went to college instead, and since I had no piano I drifted to the typewriter and banged away on those keys. I wrote short stories, had them published, and got an option from the Macmillan

Company for a novel I never finished. In between sections of the book, to cheer myself up, I wrote little fables—animal tales mostly. I found this was more fun.

I realized if I were a film person I would be a maker of short subjects, probably cartoons, not features. Meanwhile, the option (a dazzling $300) got me a summer at Princeton where I hobnobbed with writers—Phillip Roth, Mary McCarthy, poet Allen Tate and his wife Caroline Gordon. And J. Robert Oppenheimer tooled around town in a spiffy Rolls-Royce. All pretty rich stuff. I stayed in a haunted house built in 1800; doors would open and shut by themselves. Kind of nerve wracking.

A world according to Beatrix Potter was beckoning.

Macmillan's editor, Charlotte Painter, suggested I come to talk with Lee Anna Deadrick, their children's book editor. This distinguished company was the first American publisher to have a special department for children's books.

Every sensible adult said you'll never get published. What they meant to say is you'll never make money. For on the road ahead lay an even higher art form: Creative Accounting. Example: 3,000 copies sold. Yippee. Surprise—3,004 copies returned from bookstores. Result: debit of 4 copies.

Writing for kids is a form which, by nature of its brevity, demands a poet's insight, a poet's arranging and choice of words. One must say a lot in little. Say it so a child might understand and a grown-up might remember.

Was it ever true—that once upon a time I hadn't the joy of finding my name upon the cover of a book? Drift back with me to my accepting an invitation to visit the august Macmillan Company. It saw merit in my humble efforts.

> Dear Mr. Wahl,
> I like the book Humphrey's bear. It was the best book in the world. I like the book because the bear took the boy for a ride on his sailboat. The bear was the best in the book. My special stuffed animal is my elephant. I go everywhere with him I go to bed with him.
>
> Love,
> Nate

Sometimes kids write wonderful letters, with correct spelling too.

At the foot of lower Fifth Avenue lay the offices; later, spruced up, the offices of *Forbes Magazine*. At that time Macmillan was a trifle needy—just how I pictured publishing to be. Full of tradition, smelling of old books and new bindings.

Today, regretfully, publishers are part of corporate buildings, although some have moved to smaller quarters like the Flatiron Building. They give you a badge to identify you and dutifully you sign in as a guard sizes you up. Apparently, they're afraid you, disgruntled author, may blow up the establishment.

In those days, forty years ago, Macmillan indeed felt like a publisher's castle. No air conditioning, although it was summer, only asthmatic overhead ceiling fans whirring away as I climbed up the stairs feeling insignificant that afternoon. I had no trust in a rickety cage that served as an elevator to deliver me to my destination. However, I screwed up my courage when I spied two of my literary heroes hanging on the wall.

One was lyrical Irish poet William Butler Yeats. The other was noble white-bearded Indian poet Rabindranath Tagore. The photos were brown with age. Yet nodding approval—giving encouragement in the nick of time. Definitely, I was at the right place.

I was ushered into an office. Knees shook as a stern woman in a gray-starched dress and plain nurse's shoes held my future, a manuscript I'd mailed in.

She rattled pages in a bloodless bony grip. I was floating on an ice cake on the Arctic Sea and now I was going to sink or swim. For I was awaiting thumbs up or down by a severe woman in gray in that musty ancient place.

I noticed that while twisting my manuscript she began to make some sort of origami out of it. And it seemed a different hue. Had my story been dunked in coffee or tea?

I'll never forget this. Dryly, she informed me, "We" (now to this day I don't know who that *we* might be—perhaps just the royal *we* editors love to use) "like the way you write. But we..." (again—that *we*) "...at Macmillan have decided *animals don't talk*."

What I failed to reply as I slunk away was that for centuries lots of stories took for granted that animals may somehow talk. This whimsical notion goes back to Aesop or perhaps beyond. And what about Beatrix Potter? What about Toad in his roadster in *The Wind in the Willows*?

No matter. Bravely, I sent my tattered manuscript forth again. And again. Sixteen times.

The most esteemed children's department was Harper. The best illustrator, Maurice Sendak. Ah, recklessness of youth! I sent *Pleasant Fieldmouse* three times to Miss Ursula Nordstrom, boss of the department and editor of *Charlotte's Web*.

Re-entering Gotham, I booked a room at the fabled literary hangout, the Algonquin. Cost? $13 a night. I casually let Harper know I'd be there. I stepped into the elevator and out came Simone Signoret and Yves Montand. They smiled. I smiled, riding up with Jenny Hecht, daughter of Ben Hecht. Harper beckoned next morning: "Miss Nordstrom will see you."

So I arrived blinking and stammering and fiddling like Oliver Hardy with a brand-new Bloomingdale's tie as a Very Important Person greeted me.

She was as sturdy as a Mack truck. Behind those thick glasses were watchful, beady eyes. Then she growled, "*Where the hell have you been all this time?*" I decided not to mention she'd read the story twice already. Harper wasn't perfect, she boasted. "We turned down *Mary Poppins* in 1936." So I prepared for the worst.

And she added, "It's a nice length. I'll buy it! You want Sendak to illustrate? Do I scare you?"

To both questions, I nodded yes.

Later on I warmed up to her. For she admitted she too had a crush on Conrad Veidt. I gave her a handsome framed photo of him.

So I got published with many books to follow. Little did I know that my first book probably would garner the best reviews I was ever to get.

"Not since *Wind in the Willows*..." or "If you only buy one book this year make it this one..." or "...belongs on the same high shelf as Beatrix Potter."

Not bad, especially if you realize *Animals Don't Talk*.

Now we live in a visual era when pictures are given an authority we no longer give to the printed word. Therefore if one

Published at last (1964)

kid out there believes I am a good *otter*, I am thrilled. Gives me goosebumps.

And if one of my stories might be turned into a Technicolor movie starring Sabu, I would be in heaven.

Relaxing among my literary labors

Afterword
About Andrea King

I met elegant, vivacious Andrea King through a fellow Toledoan, Joe Wagstaff. Joe, in the early Thirties, made two musicals at Fox; at age eighty and counting, like the late Kitty Carlisle Hart, he continued to perform at supper clubs. At the time I met Andrea, she was living in the same apartment complex as Tab Hunter and Janis Paige, her peers at Warner Bros. She wrote her memoirs, for which, unhappily, I was unable to find a publisher. She was the star of such classics as *The Beast with Five Fingers* with Peter Lorre, *Hotel Berlin* with Raymond Massey, *Red Planet Mars* with Peter Graves and *Ride the Pink Horse*, the last opposite Robert Montgomery. The only sensational aspect of her life had been a special relationship with handsome Helmut Dantine. The publishers needed something more titillating. The last time I saw her was in company with Joe Wagstaff and Harpo Marx's son Bill, who was playing piano at a small Beverly Hills hotel. Andrea wore a stunning eggshell-hue silk pantsuit and matching silk turban—absolutely golden age Hollywood. I showed her several essays from this book while in progress and she wrote charming remarks, used in slightly different form as a Foreword to this book. With affection, I dedicated my *The Golden Christmas Tree* to her and on the day I sent her the first copy, I found her name in *The Toledo Blade* on the obituary page.

Andrea King

About the Author

Jan Wahl was born in Columbus, Ohio. His short stories and essays have appeared in *Audience, Transatlantic Review, Kosmorama, Epoch, Montage, Prairie Schooner, Films in Review* and *Films of the Golden Age*. He has won many prizes, among them the Avery Hopwood Award in Fiction, the Bologna Young Critics Prize and the Christopher Medal. He began collecting movies (on reels) and comic strip art in grade school.

CHECK THESE TITLES! BearManorMedia.com
P O Box 71426 • Albany, GA 31708 • 760-709-9696

Comic Strips and Comic Books of Radio's Golden Age
by Ron Lackmann

From Archie Andrews to Tom Mix, all radio characters and programs that ever stemmed from a comic book or comic strip in radio's golden age are collected here, for the first time, in an easy-to-read, A through Z book by Ron Lackmann!

$19.95   ISBN 1-59393-021-6

Perverse, Adverse and Rottenverse
by June Foray

June Foray, voice of Rocky the Flying Squirrel and Natasha on Rocky and Bullwinkle, has assembled a hilarious collection of humorous essays aimed at knocking the hats off conventions and conventional sayings. Her highly literate work is reminiscent of John Lennon, S.J. Pearlman, with a smattering of P.G. Wodehouse's love of language. This is the first book from the voice of Warner Brothers' Grandma (Tweety cartoons) and Stan Freberg's favorite gal!

$14.95   ISBN 1-59393-020-8

The Old-Time Radio Trivia Book
by Mel Simons

Test your OTR knowledge with the ultimate radio trivia book, compiled by long-time radio personality & interviewer, Mel Simons. The book is liberally illustrated with photos of radio stars from the author's personal collection.

$14.95   ISBN 1-59393-022-4

The Writings of Paul Frees

A full-length screenplay (The Demon from Dimension X!), TV treatments and songs written for Spike Jones—never before published rarities. First 500 copies come with a free CD of unreleased Frees goodies!

$19.95   ISBN 1-59393-011-9

How Underdog Was Born
by creators Buck Biggers & Chet Stover

The creators of Total Television, the brains behind Underdog, Tennessee Tuxedo and many classic cartoons, reveal the origin of one of cartoon's greatest champions—Underdog! From conception to worldwide megahit, the entire story of the birth of Total Television at last closes an important gap in animated television history.

$19.95   ISBN 1-59393-025-9

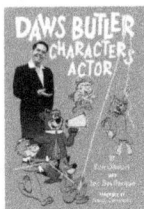

Daws Butler – Characters Actor
by Ben Ohmart and Joe Bevilacqua

The official biography of the voice of Yogi Bear, Huckleberry Hound and all things Hanna-Barbera. This first book on master voice actor Daws Butler has been assembled through personal scrapbooks, letters and intimate interviews with family and co-workers. Foreword by Daws' most famous student, Nancy Cartwright (the voice of Bart Simpson).

$24.95   ISBN 1-59393-015-1

Visit our webpage at www.bearmanormedia.com for more great deals!

They say there's nothing like a good book...

We think that says quite a lot!

BearManorMedia

P O Box 71426 • Albany, GA 31708
Phone: 760-709-9696 • Fax: 814-690-1559
Book orders over $99 always receive FREE US SHIPPING!
Visit our webpage at www.bearmanormedia.com
for more great deals!

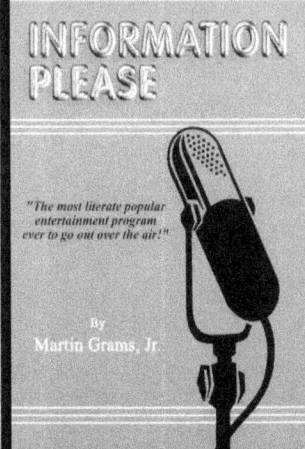

Professional typesetting, design, book & magazine layout at highly competitive rates and *FAST* turnaround. Twenty years of experience in the printing industry means having an expert on your side when dealing with printers and publishers.

Contact John Teehan at
jdteehan@sff.net
for more details.

P
rofessional typesetting, design, book & magazine layout at highly competitive rates and *FAST* turnaround. Twenty years of experience in the printing industry means having an expert on your side when dealing with printers and publishers.

Contact John Teehan at
jdteehan@sff.net
for more details.

www.ingramcontent.com/pod-product-compliance
Lightning Source LLC
Chambersburg PA
CBHW062007220426
43662CB00010B/1266